Ascendant

Modern Essays
on Polytheism and Theology

Revised Edition

Edited by Michael Hardy

BIBLIOTHECA ALEXANDRINA

Dedication

To those who ask the hard questions
and
the Powers who inspire them

Table of Contents

Introduction
Theology: What It Is, Why We Need It

by Michael Hardy

When I first began exploring polytheism as a viable religious path, sometime around 2007 or 2008, I sought out books on polytheistic theology. Theology delves into the theory of a religion, methodically developing a framework around some aspect of the tradition to explain how it works and why adherents should carry out the related practices.

When I went looking for the theology of polytheism — polytheology — I found only one book intended for the lay reader: *A World Full of Gods*, by John Michael Greer. It is an informative book, a well-argued defense of polytheism as a valid interpretation of human experience and religious impulse. But it and a few high-priced academic works were all I could find.

I found several good books on the history and development of the modern pagan movement, and I found a respectable number of basic how-to books. But there was a serious dearth of contemporary work on the underpinnings of polytheism. Since then that situation has improved somewhat, but more would certainly be welcome.

It matters because very few people today are born into polytheistic religion. Almost all of us come to it from some other religious tradition, which in the Western world, is usually some form of Christianity. Monotheistic assumptions so pervade our culture that even those polytheists who come from a non-religious background cannot help but be influenced by it. Even the "New Atheists" (who are really just old atheists with louder voices) are monotheistic atheists — they reject God, but never consider the gods of polytheism worthy of noticing at all.

The most obvious difference between monotheism and polytheism is the number of gods involved. But there is much more to it than that. The gods of polytheism are a different kind of being than the capital-G God of monotheism. Polytheism entails a very different way of understanding the world, and the divine. It raises its own questions that cannot be adequately addressed by answers originally developed in a monotheistic context. We need polytheology to explore these questions with a suitable frame of reference.

The present volume is, we hope, a useful addition to the growing body of work in this field.

From the Desk of the Editor-in-Chief

by Rebecca Buchanan

theology: the study of religious faith, practice, and experience; especially the study of God and of God's relation to the world — Merriam-Webster

polytheism: belief in or worship of more than one god — Merriam-Webster

There are two points that should be immediately noted about the above definitions. First, *theology* assumes that God is singular, and worthy of a capital G. Second, *polytheism* gets god with a lower-case g. Consulting other mainstream dictionaries produces similar results.

The bias is obvious and pervasive — so much so that modern Pagan philosophers and theologians have had to coin an entirely new term both to express exactly what they are doing, and to escape the rigid definition, assumptions, and boundaries of the previous terms.

And so we come to polytheology: *the study of religious faith, practice, and experience within a polytheistic framework; especially the study of the Gods, the Gods' relation/s to the world, and their relation/s to one another**

The creation of a new term is important, and as vital as the work itself. Modern polytheists must engage in the work of polytheology. We cannot allow others to define our beliefs and practices and experiences for us using their own terms; just consider the problems created by the translation of so many varied indigenous terms with the English words "witch" and "demon." Original meanings are lost, skewed, and transformed; practices are ignored, maligned, changed; and people are persecuted, mocked, and even executed; while whole *other* meanings — carried by the English-language terms — are applied out of context.

Polytheology is a wholly different way of engaging in theology; it is a wholly different way of understanding the Gods and their relations to one another, to the natural world, and to us. It deals with issues, concepts, and questions which are incomprehensible — even impossible — in a monotheistic cosmology.

If we as polytheists want to be understood and heard; if we want a clearer understanding for ourselves of how we fit in the world; if we want to better understand the Gods and their relationships with one another; then we must engage in polytheology — because monotheist theologians cannot, and should not, and will not understand when they do.

And because this is important work, you hold *Ascendant: Modern Essays on Polytheism and Theology* in your hands. Currently, there are very few books on polytheology available. A selection of these are listed in Appendix B: Recommended Reading. We hope that the essays here will inspire more such work, and that there will soon be many, many more books to fill the growing modern Pagan canon.

Rebecca Buchanan
Winter 2018

* I have also seen the term *theoilogy*, though far less frequently.

Why Theology?

by Wayne Keysor

Aristotle by Raphael

We all stand on a precipice, each moment of our lives ready to tumble over into the next, bringing a transformation that will inevitably define our experience for both good and ill. And we all have some little bit of control over that process, even if it is only to choose how we interpret an experience. Thus, the actions we take now and the small decisions that are the very substance of everyday life shape our overall experience in meaningful ways. For this reason, it is always important before taking up any practice to ask why? Why should we spend our time on this activity instead of that one, what do we stand to gain and lose from that choice? Theology, particularly contemporary Pagan theology, is not immune from this question. And as a practice, it is certainly open to criticism.

Contemporary Paganism is a sprawling, brawling, mewling religious movement with many conflicting and complicating strains. Although its roots go deep into western history and culture, it is a new phenomenon that is still emerging from its chrysalis. There has been no order or coherence to its outpouring, and some might say that this is exactly how it should be. Against this capacious disorder, we might pose traditional, structured, western theology as the antithesis of this organic growth, which is unordered and fundamentally incoherent in its manifestations. The practice of western theology can be defined as an attempt to bring order and coherence to our understanding of spiritual questions. It is a process in which one employs structured language to make statements about spiritual claims, then, employing the faculty of reason, to test these statements against the yardstick of logic and experience, and finally to draw valid conclusions about them. This has been the enterprise of western theology since the classical Greeks set us on our current cultural path 2,500 years ago.

Critics of this approach might argue that this path has been injurious to our daily experience of life and has ultimately led to the desiccated scientism of the modern, western world, which proudly boasts, with missionary zeal no less, that there is nothing beyond the material world, and that all moves according to understandable laws, which have nothing to do with ultimate purpose or meaning. They might further argue, with some force, that this mode of thinking has reduced the potential and possibilities of human lives, robbing them of significance, of mystery, of transcendent meaning.

Alternately, we might consider the existence of deeper spiritual truths that are not susceptible to the structured, discursive thinking that lies at the heart of human reason. This is the path of the mystic or the Avant Garde artist, who sees without logical thinking, who experiences without the need for coherent categories, who creates without the limitations of method.

Contemporary Paganism is particularly at home in this world view, as it has grown up as an "alternative religion." This is the category of the weird, of the wacky, of all the things that are not of the cultural consensus, which includes those reversals of logic and empiricism, irrationality and ecstasy. For many contemporary Pagans, it is the whole-body experience of Paganism that matters, not its underlying logic, and that experience is satisfying indeed. It has proven to be a rich, heady drink, spiked with meaning and significance, which leads the practitioner ever deeper into the mystery where all things are possible. What do chains of logic and argumentation have to offer beside the intoxicating magic of the mead of inspiration or the illumination of awen or the scintillating, energizing fire of imbas? And these are indeed valid questions which strike at the heart of our cultural legacy and the direction we want our societies to go in the future.

Can there be a defense for contemporary Pagan theology that does not undermine the arguments of the critics above, but complements them?

Let us consider that we must understand our basic nature as human beings. We indeed have spiritual, aesthetic, and emotional components to our beings, which are exactly the components that are most impoverished by modern life. These are powerful facets of our being that need to be acknowledged and cultivated in far deeper and richer capacities than they are in our current societies. However, they do not tell the whole story.

The philosopher Aristotle puts forth the claim in his famous function argument that the purpose of beings, and therefore their deepest well-being, lies in performing their highest function — the characteristic activity of that being — in an excellent fashion. For Aristotle, the characteristic activity of humans is exercising the faculty of reason. Therefore, he argues that exercising reason, defined very broadly, in accordance with virtue will bring deep human well-being, as long as one's basic physical needs are met (*Nicomachean Ethics* 1.7).

Now, one does not have to be wholly convinced by the function argument to follow Aristotle's fundamental insight that the exercise of reason is one of our defining human characteristics and is part of our basic nature. If one accepts this insight, then it becomes clear that we cannot ignore this element of our personhood without deleterious effects. Just as we have seen that to ignore the other aspects of our being has caused damage, so we would expect this to result in a similar outcome. The traveling towards spiritual understanding is a journey that needs to be approached with one's whole being, including one's rational faculties. All aspects of our personhood need to be engaged in this spiritual wandering in a deep and meaningful way, within the framework of our individual capacities, in order to have the greatest chance of success. The practice of Western theology is one way to engage the rational part of our being in this search for spiritual understanding.

At the same time, we must always be cognizant of the fact that it can never be the only way, for we must continually look to the emotional, the spiritual, and the aesthetic, to carry up our reasoning on glowing wings of imagination and possibility. We must grasp at moments of timeless time, glimpsed through wide open eyes unhindered by the mediation of structure or logic, moments when, for just one ever-expanding instant, the underlying spiritual reality asserts itself in a primal and powerful way. We must dance to the drums of our souls, which are beating out rhythms that only we can understand, but which drive us into a frenzy of whirling cloth among other dancers whose rhythms twine with our own in harmony and dissonance. Yet, I would argue that the ecstatic and the irrational works best when it is twinned with its opposite, so they might play off each other in fertile tension, drawing out insights and confusions, and pulling forth questions from the Well of Wisdom that might never have been asked otherwise.

In developing the practice of contemporary Pagan theology, we always must be careful to respect these other dimensions, to acknowledge that any reasoning, no matter how tight or well-argued, will never be the whole truth. We must also be ready to make this a truly Pagan theology, which respects multiplicity in all its dimensions. It should be a garden where that organic, disorderly flowering, which is the heart of contemporary Paganism, must not be pruned too drastically, but rather many species of theology must be able to coexist together, even if they seem contrary or clashing. This does not mean they will not be in dialogue with each other or that this dialogue will never be contentious, but we must strive to avoid becoming too fixated on truths that will never be the whole truth. Ultimately spiritual development and spiritual insight is a quest into the heart of mystery, which is never revealed just once, but is a continuing, unending series of revelations that are never exhausted. For if it was, it would not truly be mystery, and true mystery nourishes us so that we always are in the thrall of possibility, always on the verge of discovery.

Religion at its heart is a quest for mystery, and as in all quests, it is the journey that is most significant, not the destination, for the journey itself is the totality of our lived experience in this life. And as a this-worldly religion, it is that experience which we seek to cultivate. For this reason, we still can have a meaningful life even if we never discover all the fundamental spiritual truths of our universe or its overarching metaphysical principles, but we cannot have such a life if, at some level, we do not ask those questions and seek those answers. It is in the process of asking, not the answering, where true spiritual enlightenment rests. So, if we never write the grand unified theory of Paganism, we should not consider the project of contemporary Pagan theology a failure. Rather, we should remember that the goal of all our activities is to unify ourselves; reason, emotion, aesthetic senses, and spiritual sensitivity; joined together seamlessly into that one person, who is always taking that next step into the heart of mystery, the heart of revelation, with their own heart open to all the grand possibilities that life has to offer.

Works Cited

Aristotle, "Nicomachean Ethics," *The Complete Works of Aristotle: The Revised Oxford Translation, Volume Two*. Editor Jonathan Barnes. Princeton, New Jersey, Princeton University Press, 1984.

Approaching Theology
Through the Divine Individual
by Brandon Hensley

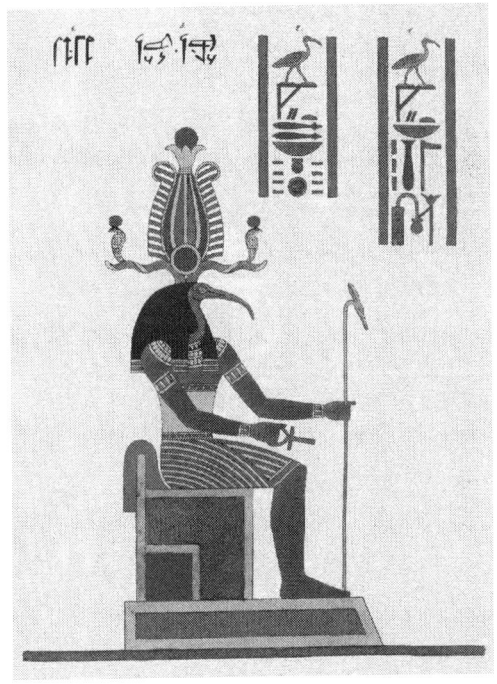

Thoout, Thoth Deux fois Grand,
le Second Hermés

Paganism is a religious tradition that is not usually associated with systematic theology. Given the general adogmatic framing of Paganism, a systematic approach to theology would appear to be incongruent; however, it is not only possible to approach Pagan theology in a systematic way, there are historical and contemporary antecedents to such a project.

As a predominantly polytheistic tradition, any discussion of Paganism would do well to focus on the gods as individuals first rather than trying to tackle the larger question of "what is a god"? To quote contemporary Pagan scholar Edward P. Butler,

Theology concerns those things first by nature according to a given philosophy. Thus, for the philosophy which takes the unit as its highest principle, theology is the study of the divine individuals, and as such concerns not what they are, but Who. (Theology)

Butler's approach to theology is rooted firmly in the tradition of the Neoplatonists, but it does reject the usual references to an all-encompassing monad, or singularity. As such, Butler's ontological approach of the divine individual will be the major focus for our definition of theology and our discussion of it.

One of the first theological debates most Pagans encounter is that of "hard polytheism" vs "soft polytheism." Even lacking the formal convictions of a theologian, every Pagan who wades into that debate is engaging in the assertion of one universal theological truth over another — therefore, engaging in theology. Generally speaking, "soft polytheism" posits that the individual gods are all really just faces of one ultimate god, while "hard polytheism" posits that the gods are all unique and individual. What is being argued is what the Classical Greeks and even early Christian writers would refer to as the first cause, and what Butler refers to when he says "those things first by nature."

A first cause is something uncreated, not material, or prior to the creation of all — i.e., the big bang. When applied to the gods, this implies something that does not have an origin in the material plane, or at least something that is not beholden to the physical laws of the universe as we know them. Sallust gives a rather succinct definition of this when he defines a god as "immutable, without Generation, eternal, incorporeal, and [without] Subsistence in Place." For our purposes, we will use the term *hyperousia*[1], from the Greek *uperteros* meaning "superior, over, or above," and *ousia*, meaning "nature, substance, essence, matter, being," et cetera. To reference the previous example: is there one *hyperousia* from which all the gods emanate and partake of? Or does each god possess their own *hyperousia* that is similar to but distinct from all others? This is the essential argument between hard and soft polytheists.

Butler also refers to another episode of this type of behavior between the Classical thinkers Iamblichus and Porphyry (Butler, 2007). Iamblichus and Porphyry were arguing whether or not the names of the gods were interchangeable — Thoth vs Hermes, for example — and whether particular meanings and idioms were implied in the original names that were not translatable into other languages, namely Greek. What is important for our discussion is that this episode illustrates the underlying assumptions of language and how it informed their ideas of diversity. Similarly, the underlying assumptions with which we load our understanding of theological concepts will inform the areas of application in which that understanding is deployed — primarily, ritual and practice.

As I explain elsewhere (Hensley, *On Dogma*, 2018), there are some self-evident dogmas, or generally accepted religious assumptions, already manifested in Pagan theology. These are: universal priesthood; orthopraxis; and the sanctity of the earth[2]. In short, Pagans do not require mediation outside themselves to experience the divine; correct action and/or behavior is preferred over correct belief or thought; and the earth is to be honored and stewarded, not disregarded and exploited. These three positions are not controversial. What tends to raise eyebrows, however, is the assertion that any given Pagan's position on these types of topics is reflective of theological dogmas. Does any given Pagan value personal experience over communal experience? Do they derive a code of ethics from the myths associated with their gods? Is the earth a manifestation of a universal whole or a particular god or goddess? Generally speaking, these questions form the basis of most Pagan discussion on the nature of our religious tradition. However, these particular questions do not fundamentally illustrate such a system, nor should they be at the root of any given theology. These questions should be treated only *after* such a system is established, if they are to be considered at all.

Referring back to Butler (2005), any universal Pagan theology would need to regard even modern non-Western Pagans as subjects of that theology.

Discrete Pagan religions require a vehicle for understanding the similar structures in their pantheons without succumbing to the notion that they are worshiping the same gods in different guises ... a method for operating entirely within a given culture's own concepts and categories to understand and express the structure their gods have given the world. (*ibid*)

Essentially what is being argued here is that Pagan theology cannot be tradition-specific, but must be a universal framework through which to examine our own relationships with the divine as well as those of others without decontextualizing them. While it is very easy to utilize Jung and a theory of archetypes in rendering all divine personality to metaphor, the thrust of a modern Pagan theology cannot regard the living traditions of other Pagan religions in such a way; therefore, to engage in consistent, good faith arguments on our own theology, it is impossible for us to regard our own as such. It is necessary then to first assume that the reality of the divine personalities, at least in the philosophical sense, is a given, and then take this assumption to examine analogous antecedents to see how we can further examine the question in the present.

Despite modern popular perceptions of the first three centuries of the Common Era, Christianity was hardly a unified monolith. Not only was this early period dominated by a variety of different Christianities (Yale, 2009), but their theological differences would pale modern exegetical differences between the hundreds of extant Christian denominations (Ehrman, 1997). As an antecedent to the Pagan discussion, the Gnostics were one of the many different versions of Christianity during this period. Gnosticism is generally defined as:

[A] religion that differentiates the evil god of this world (who is identified with the god of the Old Testament) from a higher more abstract God revealed by Jesus Christ, a religion that regards this world as the creation of a series of evil archons/ powers who wish to keep the human soul trapped in an evil physical body, a religion that preaches a hidden wisdom or knowledge only to a select group as necessary for salvation or escape from this world. (Gnostics, Gnostic Gospels, & Gnosticism)

Unfortunately for the popular consensus and the good people at Early Christian Writings, contemporary scholarship since the beginning of the twenty-first century agrees that "the Gnostics" as an organized homogeneous group did not actually exist. In his April 15, 2017 discussion on Marcion of Sinope with the Gnostic Wisdom Network, Dr. Glen Fairen explains how the traditional, easy category of "Gnostic" has given way to regarding the various groups usually contained within that umbrella as distinct entities on their own, such as the Valentinians, Johannines, and Thomasines. These same tendencies are outlined in Elaine Pagel's *The Gnostic Gospels* (she is also referenced by Fairen). What was happening in the first three centuries of the common era wasn't so much a mystery cult calling themselves the Gnostics promoting a unified, systematic theology of Jesus Christ, but a variety of groups promoting remarkably similar, yet distinct, theological systems.

Similarly, Paganism as a monolithic reinvigoration of ancient traditions is not a useful determinant for a distinct tradition. Paganism is instead a big tent phenomenon with many competing similar tendencies within it. Unfortunately, we lack the benefit of two millennia of hindsight to be able to clearly delineate these tendencies as we can with those traditionally referred to as the Gnostics; however, we can make some rough generalizations. The most basic delineation is Organized/Lineaged vs Eclectic/Solitary. The Organized Pagans tend to resemble traditional religious organizations with established priesthoods, hierarchies, creeds, rituals, liturgies, et cetera, while the Eclectic with its many different and unique amalgamations of traditions and practices tends to be more intimately familiar to the average, contemporary Pagan. In the latter category, there tends to be a great overlap of source material and even overlaps between pantheons. Despite these differences in approach between the two major demographics of Paganism, there is an underlying constant to these two general camps. There is a restoration of what was but in a modern context (to quote a dear friend: "We are the modern children of the ancient gods."), and a rejection of Christian doctrinal orthodoxy and the associated cultural detritus. The specific forms these theologies take is largely dependent on the cultures and historic remnants claimed by the Pagan in question as filtered through their individual contemporary worldview — i.e., a Celtic Witch who practices Gardnerian circle-casting and utilizes new age crystal grids vs a Roman Reconstructionist who seeks to emulate as faithfully as possible the historic practice as related in archaeological and textual remains. This postmodern approach to religion has many benefits for anyone who is seeking to keep themselves out of the general line of sight of doctrinal orthodoxy, but this may not be entirely possible and actually creates more problems than it solves.

One major point of contention is the role of cultural appropriation in Paganism writ large. By not treating our own gods as more than just a sum of our personal experiences with them, we rid ourselves of the responsibility in treating other gods in their own context. The dominant postmodern view in Paganism lacks any explanatory or analytic capacity when it comes to how we interact with the divine. The adage "ask ten Pagans their definition of Paganism and get thirteen answers," while humorous, is indicative of the shortcomings of this approach in general and its lack of analytical capacity in particular. It also underscores the need for a positive alternative to the Pagan status quo. The debates between the Gnostics and the proto-Orthodox Neoplatonists are similar to what is playing out in Paganism now. Unfortunately, the Gnostic philosophy, in rejecting the material world, lacked any efficient explanatory capacity while Neoplatonism was, and is, rooted in an expectation that the natural world around us can be explained and understood in real terms. Ultimately Postmodernism (and Paganism) cannot continue endlessly reducing reality to meaningless language games (Gibbons, 2017). Reality exists regardless of one's experience of it. Postmodern approaches to Paganism will eventually give way to more material metaphysics — the question is how will we define our own myths and ontologies to engage in these questions of faith in the present world once Postmodernism is finally usurped?

Butler's approach relies on the reading of myth as the equivalent of revealed text. In his preface to *Essays on a Polytheistic Philosophy of Religion*, he points out that questions of theological interpretation and exegesis tends to be pedagogically exclusive to Abrahamic religions both in academia and in the wider public. Because of this, even among Pagans who nominally take on these various pantheons as their own, this type of interpretation and speculative theology characteristic of mainstream religions is absent. Myth is relegated to the academic, historic, and anachronistic. Its value as living text to inform modern tradition is relegated to the dustbin of superstition. Similarly to our previous discussion on the necessary living reality of the gods, it should be accepted without controversy that the treatment of myth should likewise be treated in real terms. Just as we cannot in good faith regard the traditional religions of indigenous peoples as purely academic metaphors from the past, consistency demands that we treat our own mythic texts with greater seriousness than we currently do. This absolutely does not require a literal belief in the contents of myth. Just as only a fringe of the Christian religious believe in a literal seven days of creation, there is no reason a mature Pagan theology cannot reasonably engage in the myths of our gods as seriously as Christian scholars engage with the Bible.

To illustrate the nature of how this would work, we can borrow Butler's approach in treating the divine personalities as individuals (and by extension, their related myths) and focus on the role and exegesis of a particular god — Thoth. In the Egyptian cycle of myths, Thoth is present in the theology devised at Hermopolis (Egyptian: *Khemenu*) when he laid the world egg on the primordial hill. The egg hatched revealing Ra who then created the world and everything in it. By treating Thoth and this myth as *real* in a philosophical sense, and treating Thoth and Ra as unique individuals therein, what develops is a particular relation between the two. Thoth exists before the universe is materially created. Ra is the creator, the demiurge, responsible for the material world while Thoth exists prior to and outside of it. Thoth's subsequent roles in the drama between Set and Osiris sees him, once again, playing kingmaker just as he placed Ra at the head of creation when he allows Osiris to violate the universal cycle of life and death and become king of the underworld, then once again when he assists both Set and Horus in their battle over the inheritance of Osiris (much to the consternation of Ra who must routinely call the council of gods together while unable to make a definitive ruling one way or the other).

Thoth therefore represents, among many other things, an innate tension between the material limitations of the physical and the spiritual endeavors of the mystical. This exegesis can then be read back into the text in his additional roles to derive yet additional layers of meaning. For instance, Thoth existing prior to the material world highlights his choice to enter the created world and play a part in the courts of the various gods. What does this imply about the role of language and writing? What does Thoth's principle role in the court of Osiris at the judgment of the dead say about his relation to Ra and the material world?

This small example is just an insight into what this system of Pagan theology could engage in. The creation myth of Hermopolis is not treated literally. The juxtaposition of Thoth and Ra (and the Osirian narrative, by extension) at the inception of the universe sets the stage for how we understand their roles in later places where they both appear and goes far in how we read and comprehend these myths. They then allow us a convenient avenue to devise meaning from them for our present lives.

The second benefit to this approach is in answering a far better-equipped community that sees their principle theological impetus as the saving of others from their own god — the Evangelical Christians. The Pew Research Center in 2015 showed an exceptional increase in the number of Evangelical Protestants in the United States juxtaposed against an overall decline in Christian religious. In January 2018, *The Federalist* magazine released an article indicating that discrepancies in narratives between the growth of Evangelicalism and the overall decline of Christianity can be explained by "the intensity and seriousness with which people hold and practice [their] faith." (Stanton, 2018) Part of the strength of the Evangelical movement ultimately comes from a commonly held framework of theological interpretation and application. Even as different congregations may engage in different exegetical conclusions, the overall exegetical framework and hermeneutic is similar enough to be the same.

One of the primary outlets through which Evangelicals gather their data and arguments is the Christian Apologetics Resource Ministry (CARM). Compiled and edited by Matt Slick, CARM is a clearinghouse of questions, answers, and tactics for evangelizing. One of the more telling techniques explained by Slick is included under the heading "Witnessing to Those in Wicca":[3]

Learn what he/she believes in by asking questions. There are different traditions within Wicca and what you learn from one may not necessarily agree in every aspect with another Wiccan. Therefore, it is absolutely necessary that you ask questions. There's nothing wrong with learning what it is that they do and why they believe what they believe. I find that asking questions is one of the best things you can do when talking to anybody in any different theological system. I ask questions, listen intently to the answers, and then ask more questions. Invariably I begin to discover inconsistencies in their answers and I politely ask more questions around those inconsistencies. It does not take long for the person to start seeing that their belief system has serious problems. Remember, anything that is not based on the Christian faith is false and will have errors which you can discover through asking questions.

It should be clear from the last line that CARM is not encouraging good-faith dialogue with those who are not their fellow coreligionists. This tactical questioning is designed to undermine confidence and conviction. While the average Christian, Evangelical or not, is not going to be a theological scholar any more than the average Pagan, the average lay Christian is in a far better prepared place to begin this sort of conversation than their Pagan counterpart. While non-engagement is always an option, the number of sites, blogs, and editorials defending Paganism against charges of devil-worship is testament enough to Pagans' good faith willingness to engage and educate, so we should be prepared to do so whenever possible. To borrow an adage from the political Left: "Talk to them or someone else will." It is an imperative that we choose engagement when we can.

To this end, the development of a consistent theological system answers a particular need in regards to the long term viability of any Pagan project. In many respects, a nascent theology is already growing organically. But even the most organic vegetables do better with close attention and careful tending. Likewise, a Pagan theology will require equally careful tending. Despite Paganism's tendency toward the adogmatic and unorthodox, there is no reasonable concern that systematic theology should take the same route as historic Christianity. In fact, it is very likely that this fear of monolithic orthodoxy is just a shibboleth. There is no "Pax Romana" or Emperor Constantine to adopt and enforce Paganism as a world political doctrine. There will be no Pagan Nicaea. The conditions for such a path for Paganism simply do not exist in the modern world, and it is likely such conditions never will. Just as the classical Pagans had multiple cosmological realities and competing theologies, so should we expect the same for modern Paganism.

This framing of the gods as individuals within their own context and possessing their own holistic myth cycles creates an ontological framework that allows us to not only engage in the gods of pre-Christian Europe and the ancient Near East, but even to come to grips with pagan traditions that have a contiguous connection with their own ancient counterparts in a serious, respectful way. It renders particular questions — notably the hard polytheism vs soft polytheism debate — inconceivable (Butler, 2008), and opens us up to new, much more eminently practical questions such as "what is a Pagan system of ethics," and "how do we as Pagans engage politically and socially," among others.

Regardless of the paths Paganism takes, to pretend that Paganism can exist free of doctrinal concerns and theological systems is a fool's errand. Through the work of people like Edward P. Butler, John Opsopaus, Michael York, and others, we find the Pandora's Box of theological speculation to be forever opened. The only option once the box *is* opened is to accept or reject what it contains. But, if rejected, a positive alternative is required. Like the debates of the Rabbinical Mishnah and the

Neoplatonists, so too will the great Pagan debate move forward.

Works Cited

Butler, E. P. "The Theological Interpretation of Myth," *The Pomegranate: The International Journal of Pagan Studies*, 2005. *7*(1), 27-41.

Butler, E. P. "Offering to the Gods: A Neoplatonic Perspective," *Magic, Ritual, and Witchcraft*, 2007. *2*(1), 1-20.

Butler, E. P. "Polycentric Polytheism and the Philosophy of Religion," *The Pomegranate: The International Journal of Pagan Studies*, 2008. *10*(2), 207-229.

Butler, E. P., *Essays on a Polytheistic Philosophy of Religion.* New York, Phaidra Editions, 2014.

Butler, E. P. "Theology," *Henadology*, n.d. https://henadology.wordpress.com/theology/

Ehrman, B. D. *The New Testament: A historical introduction to the early Christian writings.* New York, Oxford University Press, 1997.

Gibbons, A. "Postmodernism is dead. What comes next?" *The Times Literary Supplement*, 2017. https://www.the-tls.co.uk/articles/public/postmodernism-dead-comes- next/

[Gnostic Wisdom Network]. (2017, April 15) [Talk Gnosis] Marcion of Sinope [Video File]. Retrieved from https://www.youtube.com/watch?v=B-zjOTFGA7c

Hensley, B. "On Dogma," *An Examen of Witches*, 2018. https://anexamenofwitches.wordpress.com/2018/01/24/on-dogma/

Pagels, E. H. *The Gnostic Gospels*, New York, Vintage Books, 1989.

Pew Research Center, *America's Changing Religious Landscape*, 2015. http://www.pewforum.org/2015/05/12/americas-changing-religious-landscape/

Sallust, *On the Gods and the World*, n.d.

Slick, Matt, "Witnessing to those in Wicca," *Christian Apologetics Resource Ministry*, 2011. https://carm.org/witnessing-to-those-in-wicca

Stanton, G. T. "New Harvard Research Says U.S. Christianity Is Not Shrinking, But Growing Stronger," *The Federalist*, 2018.
http://thefederalist.com/2018/01/22/new-harvard-research-says-u-s-christianity-not-shrinking-growing-stronger/

Unbylined, "Gnostics, Gnostic Gospels, & Gnosticism," *Early Christian Writings*, n.d. http://www.earlychristianwritings.com/gnostics.html

[Yale Courses]. (2009, September 2). 5. The New Testament as History [Video File]. Retrieved from address https://www.youtube.com/watch?v=BQaOlxhg8xg&list=PL462B0F2345C29AFA&index=5

The One and the Many:
An Essay on Pagan Neoplatonism

by John Michael Greer

Plato's Academy (mosaic in Pompeii)

The contemporary renaissance of polytheism in the Western world has a complex relationship to its own past. Most of those involved in today's rising polytheist movements see themselves as returning to ancient roots, recovering a primal spirituality that thrived before the arrival of Christianity.

However, those ancient roots are often simply fabricated — new religions masquerading as the Old Religion are common these days — and even when they aren't, the use of ancient traditions by modern polytheists tends to be highly selective.

Such a smorgasbord approach to tradition, to be sure, is all but universal in the history of religions. Symbols, practices, and philosophies are routinely discarded and replaced by others as the generations pass, for reasons ranging from the serious to the whimsical, and sometimes what was discarded by one generation is picked up by another and put back into use. The revival of polytheism as an authentic religious option in our time, in fact, is a classic example of this process at work.

A case can always be made, then, for raids on the past in the service of spiritual renewal. This essay may be seen as an attempt to incite such a raid — in the spirit, perhaps, of some ancient Pictish bard rousing the warriors with song before they went off to climb over Hadrian's Wall and plunder the Romans. The target of the raid I have in mind is a tradition of philosophy that provided the core theological basis for Pagan religious practice in the classical world during the last three centuries or so of its struggle for survival against political Christianity and was revived in the Renaissance and then again in the early nineteenth century along with the classical Paganism it supported.

The tradition in question, of course, is Neoplatonism. As a set of tools for understanding polytheist religious discourse and practice, Neoplatonism has a long and distinguished history. and this makes it an obvious target for a revival of the sort discussed above. Such a revival is useful because too many of today's polytheists have uncritically adopted theological approaches from Christianity, which are designed to support a dogmatic scriptural monotheism and are often poorly suited to the very different needs of today's diverse polytheist revivals.

Too many people in contemporary polytheist movements, however, dismiss Neoplatonism out of hand. As far as I know, no survey has been done on the subject, but such anecdotal data as I have been able to gather suggests that among those of today's polytheists who have heard of Neoplatonism at all, most reject it for one of two reasons. On the one hand, it is seen as monotheist — that is, affirming a belief in one and only one god, compared to whom all other deities can only be lesser beings, incomplete manifestations, or ignorant misunderstandings on the part of human worshipers.

On the other hand, it is seen as monist —

that is, committed to a view of the world in which all things come from and return to an undifferentiated oneness.

Neither of these is an accurate description of Neoplatonism. Both misunderstandings follow on specific events in the history of Neoplatonism and the broader history of ideas in the Western world. Thus, a glance back over the history of Neoplatonism will help set the stage for a clearer understanding of Neoplatonism as a polytheist religious philosophy — the role it had during the last golden autumn of classical Paganism, and during both major revivals of classical Paganism in the Western world before the twentieth century.

A Brief History of Neoplatonism

As the name suggests, the story of Neoplatonism starts with the philosopher Aristocles of Athens (429-347 BCE), whose very broad shoulders earned him the nickname Plato (from the Greek *platon*, broad.) A brilliant writer as well as an incisive thinker, Plato crafted a series of dialogues that tackled most of the significant issues of Greek philosophy, which in turn kickstarted a process of inquiry that led straight to the Pagan Neoplatonic theology of a later era.

Central to the Greek philosophical project were questions about what actually exists in the world we experience, and the early Greek philosophers — the Presocratics, as they are usually called — by and large tried to come up with one-size-fits-all answers. Plato pointed out, in contrast, that we encounter at least two different kinds of existing things. We encounter material things — things with weight, color, and other sensory properties — but these don't exhaust the world we experience.

Consider a mathematical equation such as 1 + 1 = 2. While it can be expressed in material form — say, by writing it in ink on a piece of paper — the equation is not a material thing. It can be known in the mind, as a purely mental experience. That mental experience, furthermore, touches something real. Compare the equation 1 + 1 = 2 to such not-really-equations as 1 + 1 = 3 and 1 + 1 = @, and the "something real" is easier to grasp. 1 + 1 = 2 expresses a truth; those who grasp that truth can derive other truths from it and apply those truths to the world of material things.

Plato thus argued that human beings live at the intersection of two worlds: a world of facts that can be known by the senses, and a world of truths that can be known by the mind. He argued further that the world of truths — in his terms, the world of Forms or Ideas — was the source of the world of facts, that each material thing we see is an imperfect reflection of mental truths.

Most people in modern industrial society insist on seeing things the other way around and think of mental truths as abstractions based on material facts. The conventional wisdom was not that different in Plato's time, which is why his dialogues explore the relation between the world of truths and the world of facts from so many different angles. Counterintuitive as it seems from our modern perspective, Plato's approach works well in practice, and proved to be a fertile source of new philosophical insights. After Plato's time, as a result, many other philosophers picked up where he left off and explored the relationship between facts and truths in more detail.

Neoplatonism itself emerged out of these further explorations. It was launched by the Greek-Egyptian philosopher Plotinus (204-270 CE), who taught at Rome and whose lectures were collected by his pupil Porphyry as The Enneads. Plotinus took the two worlds described by Plato and argued that their existence requires the existence of two more worlds — or, to put the same insight in a different way, two other kinds of existing things.

There are, to begin with, minds that perceive the world of facts and the world of truths. Minds also perceive a realm of their own — a realm that consists of thoughts, feelings, memories, mental imagery, and the like. Thus, between the world of facts and the world of truths, Plotinus posited a world of individual minds or personalities, which can face in either direction, toward facts and the world of matter and change, or toward truths and the world of enduring realities.

The fourth world is harder to describe in simple terms because under normal conditions, our minds have no direct contact with it. In certain mystical states, we encounter a ground of being or basic principle of existence; certain abstruse philosophical reasonings argue for the existence of the same thing, which is not a truth, a person, or a fact, but something else. Plotinus referred to it as "the One," and spent many of his lectures showing that it did not belong to any of the other three worlds and did not share any of their characteristic qualities. Thus the Neoplatonist universe has four levels or kinds of being: the hylic level, the world of material facts; the psychic level, the world of individual minds; the noetic level, the world of timeless truths; and the henadic level, which consists solely of the One.

The One, in this scheme, is the source of existence and the ground of being. The noetic level comes into being as a response to the One, the psychic level comes into being in response to the noetic level, and the hylic level comes into being in response to the psychic level, in a cascade of creation that results finally in the complex world of facts, minds, and truths we encounter. None of the other levels, and nothing that exists on any of these levels, is "part of" the One, for the One has no parts. Any attempt to describe the One in terms of the worlds below it, using concepts appropriate to an idea, a person, or a material thing, is by definition a falsification. Strictly speaking, the One cannot even be said to exist — rather, it is the principle through which existence comes into being.

Plotinus' reasoning had an immense impact on the classical world, and his Neoplatonism gradually became the default option for classical philosophers. It also became, half a century after his death, the intellectual basis for the Pagan resistance to the rising power of political Christianity. Long before then, Plotinus himself challenged the world-hating movement of Gnosticism in one of the essays collected in *The Enneads*, and Plotinus' student Porphyry wrote an essay titled *Against the Christians* which shredded the philosophical and historical claims of Christian theologians. (Not surprisingly, every copy of Porphyry's essay was burnt once Christians seized power in the Roman world; we know about its contents only from brief references in other works.)

Far more significant in his impact was Iamblichus (c. 250-325 CE), the most influential Neoplatonist after Plotinus himself. Iamblichus was a devout worshiper of the Pagan gods, as well as a capable philosopher, and he made it his life's work to bridge the remaining gaps between Neoplatonism and classical Pagan religion. The theology he outlined, which was developed much more completely by later Neoplatonists, will receive attention later in this essay; the point relevant here is that Iamblichus' revision of Neoplatonism came to be accepted almost universally as the philosophical basis and justification for Pagan religious practice during the final struggle for survival against the Christians.

While that struggle ended in defeat, most of the core Neoplatonist writings survived intact, including *The Enneads*, some of Porphyry's and Iamblichus' writings, and many of the writings of Proclus, the last great classical Pagan Neoplatonist, who set out the teachings of the school in great detail. During the Renaissance, these writings were translated into Latin by a variety of scholars and sparked a significant resurgence of interest in classical Paganism. In the late eighteenth and early nineteenth centuries, in turn, they were translated into English by Thomas Taylor (1758-1835), a devout worshiper of the ancient Greek gods and the founding father of the modern polytheist revival. In both cases, though, the potential impact of Neoplatonism was blunted by confusions between Neoplatonist ideas and other, superficially similar concepts, first from Christianity and then from points further east.

Christian and Orientalist Misinterpretations

As organized Christianity seized political power in the late Roman world, its followers found their religion stigmatized by educated Romans as an ignorant superstition without any serious intellectual foundation. One common gambit taken by Christian intellectuals in response to these charges was to borrow the ideas of Neoplatonism, by then far and away the most popular philosophical school in the Roman world. Christian Neoplatonism, the tradition that emerged from this borrowing, went on to become the foundation of Christian theology for the first thousand years or so of Christian history; it still has that status in the Eastern Orthodox churches, though it was replaced by the Christian Aristotelianism of Thomas Aquinas in the Catholic church, and by a variety of more recent philosophies in most of the Protestant world.

The Christian interpretation of Neoplatonism thus became extremely widespread in the Western world, and has shaped (or, more exactly, misshaped) a great many attempts to understand Neoplatonism from the Renaissance onward. The difficulty here is that Christian Neoplatonism is an attempt to unite two essentially incompatible systems of thought. We have already seen that Neoplatonism grounds existence in a transcendent impersonal principle, the One. According to Christian theology, the foundation of existence is not a principle but a deity, the Christian god, who is understood as a divine person with thoughts, intentions, and emotions such as love and jealousy. This divine person, to Christians, is the ultimate source and sustainer of all things.

Christian Neoplatonists insisted (and still insist) that their god is the same as the One described by Plotinus and the Pagan Neoplatonists. They had to do this because, as we will see later in this essay, Neoplatonism is inherently polytheist. As the ground of being and principle of existence, the One is the only thing in the Neoplatonist cosmos of which there can only be one. To define the god of Christianity as a god in the terms of classic Neoplatonism would be to make him simply one god among many, or at best, the only god who happens to exist (rather than, as Christian theology requires, the only god who can exist). Only by claiming that the Christian god is also the One, the unique ground of being and principle of existence, could Christian Neoplatonists claim for their god the role that their theology demands for him.

The difficulty, of course, is that in Neoplatonism, the One is not and cannot be a person. Persons belong to the third or psychic level of being, not to the first or henadic level. To claim that the One of Neoplatonism is a deity who is loving, angry and jealous, chooses a single human ethnic group as his chosen people, and has a son who incarnates as a human being to save humanity from its sins, is thus precisely the same kind of absurdity as claiming that the concept of mathematical equality is bright orange, smells of vinegar, and weighs exactly thirty-two pounds. The attempts of Christian Neoplatonists to evade or justify this absurdity make an interesting chapter in intellectual history, but do not concern us here.

The point relevant to the present discussion is that the absurdity just mentioned remains fixed in place in the minds of many people who encounter Neoplatonism. The Renaissance revival of Neoplatonism in particular helped accomplish the fixing. One of the central themes of comparative religion during the Renaissance was the belief that all the intellectual legacies of antiquity were fragments of a primordial wisdom given to humanity at the beginning of time. Since Christian theology and the Jewish Cabala were among the traditions believed to descend from that source, the Judeo-Christian concept of ultimate reality as a divine person became a Procrustean bed into which the very different legacy of Pagan Neoplatonism was forced, via a great deal of lopping and stretching.

The legacy of Thomas Taylor and the nineteenth-century Pagan revival he set in motion suffered a different fate, though one equally productive of confusion. Taylor's influential translations of the Pagan Neoplatonists appeared in print just as the Western world was becoming aware of the immense philosophical and mystical heritage of India. Central to many schools of Hindu philosophy is the belief that all multiplicity is ultimately an illusion, that the multitude of apparent things in the universe are all temporary and illusory forms taken by a single transcendent unity (Purusha or Brahman). The most influential of the classical

Hindu philosophical schools thus embrace a strict monism. This aspect of Hindu thought was taken up with great enthusiasm by such Western thinkers as Ralph Waldo Emerson, who saw in it a healthy counterbalance to the arid Christian sectarianism of their time.

It was almost inevitable in that context that the Neoplatonist writings of Plotinus, Iamblichus, and Proclus would be interpreted through an Orientalist filter, and the One of Neoplatonism would therefore be equated to the Purusha of the Hindu philosophers and mystics. A close reading of the Neoplatonists, and especially of Iamblichus, might have forestalled this, but for a variety of reasons such close readings were rare at the time. As a result, most of those readers of Neoplatonist writings who failed to misinterpret the One as a god, and thus mistook Neoplatonism for a monotheist philosophy, proceeded to misinterpret the One as the whole of which all things are parts, and thus mistook Neoplatonism for a monist philosophy.

It is unfortunate that the discovery of Hindu philosophy in the early nineteenth century was not accompanied at that same time by a discovery of Chinese philosophy. The concept of Tao, central to most of the classic Chinese schools of philosophy, would have provided Western thinkers with a much better correspondence to Neoplatonist thought than anything in Hindu philosophy, because the Tao, like the One, is a principle rather than a person. The Tao is not a god, nor is the Tao an undifferentiated oneness out of which all things come and to which all things return. The Tao is simply "the way things happen." It is the principle by which things come into being. Unfortunately for the history of Neoplatonism, the discovery of Taoism by Western thinkers came much later, when Taylor's works had dropped out of fashion.

Getting beyond the paired misunderstandings just described will be necessary if Neoplatonism is to be restored to its traditional place as a meaningful option for polytheist theology. To accomplish this, we can start with a straightforward question: in the Pagan Neoplatonism of Iamblichus and his heirs, what is a god?

The Gods of Neoplatonism

Iamblichus himself answered this in an intriguing way, starting from the nature of the individual human being. Each of us, in Neoplatonic terms, is embodied in a material form, the body, which belongs to the hylic level of being. Each of us in turn has an individual mind and personality, the soul, which belongs to the psychic level of being. This much, most people realize even today.

The Neoplatonist analysis, however, does not end there. To all the Neoplatonists, each of us also has an essential form or idea, which is the foundation of our existence. This is the spirit, which belongs to the noetic level of being. This threefold structure, in turn, depends for its existence on the presence of the One, but the One is in no way part of the self, nor is the self in any sense part of the One — the One, again, has no parts, nor can it be cut up and distributed among selves like so many slices of cake at a birthday party.

This analysis is shared, with minor variations, by all the Neoplatonic writers. The genius of Iamblichus was to take the perspectives of classical polytheism and apply this analysis to the beings revered by devout Pagans in his time and ours. Hellenic Pagans made offerings to a great many beings, which were traditionally divided into three broad classes: gods, daimons, and heroes. These three form a spectrum of being of a sort found quite commonly in traditional polytheisms: gods are the primary powers of the cosmos, daimons are less potent and more localized spiritual beings, and heroes are human beings who by their deeds in life have become touched with sacred power and continue to act as protectors and guides after death. (The Christian classification of God, the angels, and the saints is a variant of the same classical system, borrowed without acknowledgment and reworked in various ways for the purposes of Christian theology.)

To Iamblichus, the individual human being is the fourth and lowest part of this same sequence.

In a series of proportions of a kind Neoplatonists delighted to use, as we are to heroes, heroes are to daimons, and daimons are to gods. Thus, the same relationship to the levels of being that we find in ourselves, in a small way, is present also in the gods, in a superlative way.

From the Neoplatonic perspective, in other words, the gods also have spirits, souls, and bodies. Some gods, indeed, have material bodies. In ancient Greece, for example, one common way to talk about wet weather was to say, "Zeus is raining." To the Greeks, in other words, the atmosphere was in some sense the body of Zeus; Demeter's body was the soil, Poseidon's the ocean, Hestia's the fire upon the hearth, and so on. Other gods have bodies of other kinds, and these need not be limited to any form we are capable of perceiving — or conceiving.

In late Pagan Neoplatonist theology, building on this latter idea, philosophers drew a distinction between encosmic gods — those who have material bodies and exist within the world of matter as we know it — and hypercosmic gods — those who have bodies of a kind we cannot comprehend, and exist outside of matter as we know it. This distinction was created specifically for the purposes of understanding the theology of the ancient Greek and Hellenistic Mysteries, and may or may not be relevant to other traditions, but it shows the flexibility with which a Neoplatonist approach can deal with variations in deity.

In addition to a body, each god also has a soul — that is, a mind and personality, with its own thoughts, emotions, memories, and will — and a spirit, an eternal essence or nature that is the foundation of its existence. Each god also has a relationship to the One, the ground of being, just as every other existing being does. All these distinctions are equally true of daimons and heroes. A dryad, for example — the indwelling spirit of a sacred tree — has a body, which is that of the tree; a soul, which is the mind and personality that indwells the tree and the space around it, being less limited in its powers than those of human beings; a spirit, which is its essential idea or form; and a relation to the One.

And the One? Once again, the One is not a god. It does not have a spirit, a soul, or a body. It is simply the principle by which all things exist. It is what exists on the henadic level of being, the way that ideas exist on the noetic level, minds exist on the psychic level, and material objects exist on the hylic level. A god, by contrast, is a being composed of things on three of those levels, with a necessary relation to the fourth. (The same can be said of a human being; the difference, of course, is that humans are at the smallest, weakest, and simplest end of a vast spectrum of beings, and the gods are at the other end of that spectrum.) The One, then, is part of the landscape of the cosmos, like truths, minds, and material things; the gods are those great figures who bestride the landscape thus described.

Neoplatonism and Polytheist Theology

The advantages of this approach to a modern polytheist theology are clear. From a Neoplatonist standpoint, it is a needless waste of time to try to turn the gods of Pagan polytheism into a collection of petty Jehovahs, burdened with the impossible task of functioning as the ground of being and the principle of existence while remaining individual beings with bodies, minds, and spirits. The One, the principle by which things exist, supplies the universe with its ground of being, and thus leaves the gods free to be in theology what they are in reality. Since the One is not a god, has no myths, and receives no worship, it can be left to the contemplation of philosophers and mystics, while ordinary worshipers can do as polytheists have always done, and establish mutually beneficial relationships with those superlative beings we call gods.

From a Neoplatonist perspective, such relationships are natural and normal. The universe of Pagan Neoplatonism is a vast community inhabited by countless beings of many different kinds, all of which exist in three worlds and have a relationship to the fourth. In a human community, it is normal for most individuals to establish close personal relationships with certain other human beings, but not with all. In the same way, in the wider community of the cosmos, it is normal for most human beings to establish close personal relationships with certain gods, and/or with certain of the beings intermediate between the gods and humanity, but not with all.

Equally, in a human community, it is common for people to seek protection from the strong, guidance from the wise, and nurturing from the loving. The same principle applies equally well to relations between humans and the beings that the classical Pagan Neoplatonists classified as gods, daimons, and heroes. Since gods and human beings, at the extreme ends of the spectrum of conscious personhood, differ in kind but not in essential nature, such relationships are just as natural as relationships among human beings; in both cases, they are not required by the nature of things, but important dimensions of human life shrivel if they are neglected.

From a Neoplatonist perspective, further-more, it is obvious that there are many gods, and that they differ at least as much from one another as humans differ from one another. The only level of being that has only one thing in it is the henadic level, and of beings who combine spirit, soul, and body into a working unity, the universe is as full as it can be; as the Presocratic philosopher Thales is said to have remarked, "all things are full of gods." Since the One is the principle of existence, not a monotheistic "overgod" of which all gods are bite-sized servings or a monistic unity that cooks down all beings into an undifferentiated paste, gods, daimons, heroes, and human beings remain unique, individual entities — as indeed we find them to be.

From a Neoplatonist perspective, finally, the sort of literalist interpretation of mythology that has caused so much pointless folly in dogmatic scriptural religions is ruled out from the start. As the Neoplatonist philosopher Sallust put it, "myths are things that never happened, but always are." Myths, in other words, are stories communicated by gods to human beings in order to help us understand something of the noetic level, which gods perceive far more clearly than we do. They are not statements of historical fact — that is, of events on the hylic level — though they can sometimes be echoed by material events of various kinds. They are not statements about psychological archetypes — that is, of things on the psychic level — though they are often echoed by psychological processes of various kinds. Nor, finally, do they have anything to do with the One. They are expressions in narrative form of timeless realities of the noetic level, the world of forms or ideas from which the worlds of mind and matter receive their meaning and purpose.

One final note may be worth making in this context. Nothing in Pagan Neoplatonist theology requires Pagan Neoplatonist theology to be the only option when it comes to trying to understand the gods. Dogmatism in general fits very poorly in any polytheist worldview; faiths that accept the reality of many gods rarely have any difficulty accepting the validity of many differing narratives, theologies, and interpretations of the gods. While Pagan Neoplatonism became almost universally accepted among Pagans in the late Roman world, this was driven by the need to unite in the face of political Christianity, and the widely-shared conviction that at that time, Neoplatonism offered the strongest and most convincing justifications for traditional Pagan faith and practice.

In earlier centuries, by contrast, lively philosophical debates between many contending schools of thought had been a constant feature of classical intellectual life. Platonists, Aristotelians, Stoics, Epicureans, and members of yet other philosophical schools contended against one another with the same enthusiasm — and in much the same spirit — as athletes did in the various sacred games. Neoplatonism was a robust contender in the former competitions. As the modern revival of polytheism begins to explore the possibilities of a theology free from the problems and pre-suppositions of scriptural monotheism, a renewed Pagan Neoplatonism provides one direction in which theological explorations might productively unfold.

Further Reading

The best introduction to Pagan Neo-platonism for modern readers is Gregory Shaw's *Theurgy and the Soul: The Neoplatonism of Iamblichus* (Pennsylvania State University Press, 1995). On a less academic level, many of the writings of American occultist and Neoplatonist Manly P. Hall are valuable; his pamphlet series *Neoplatonism: Theology for Wanderers in the New Millennium*, based on a 1983 lecture series, is particularly recommended.

Of the classic works of Neoplatonist philosophy, Plotinus' *The Enneads* is available in many good translations. Less widely available but well worth study are Iamblichus' *On the Mysteries*, his most important exploration of the common ground between Neoplatonist philosophy and ancient polytheist worship; Sallust's *On the Gods and the World*, a primer of Neoplatonist Paganism from the era of Emperor Julian's revival of traditional Greek religion, and Proclus' *The Elements of Theology*, which sets out the logic of classical Greek worship based on an elaborately developed Neoplatonism.

Two Models of Polytheism

by Edward P. Butler

Vyasa Grants Sanjaya a Divine Vision

Polytheism, William James once said, is a term which "usually gives offense".[1] Unfortunately, this is scarcely less true today than when he said it more than a century ago. Academic discourse having grown more subtle, however, in the interim, we are more likely today to encounter the claim that polytheism in effect never existed at all, or scarcely ever, than to meet with the direct denunciation of polytheism as ignorant, incoherent, and doomed to supersession.

"Polytheism," we are told, is a term that originates in Christian polemics and hence is ripe for deconstruction. This assertion is, in the first place, debatable, inasmuch as a cursory search of Liddell and Scott's lexicon shows that forms of the word are attested as early as Aeschylus.

Beyond this, however, and as a rule of thumb, we ought to beware of the deconstructive tendency when it is turned toward the subordinated term in an opposition and deployed in such a fashion as to strengthen the term which is already hegemonic. We live in a world in which monotheism is hegemonic and has been for a very long time. In such an environment, it is entirely possible to find everywhere one turns the mere illusion of debate, in which both sides tacitly shore up the hegemonic ideology, however bitter their

---

[1] William James, *A Pluralistic Universe* (New York: Longmans, Green and Co., 1909), p. 310.

differences on matters that do not fundamentally affect the values and presuppositions shared by both sides. Monotheism, I would argue, is not merely an *instance* of such a hegemonic ideology, but is the paradigm of all of them, totalizing ideologies of every kind having been informed and shaped by monotheistic polemics spread throughout the world by Christian power both hard and soft, including in manifold secular guises. Under such circumstances, if we are to stake any claim to intellectual honesty and integrity, extraordinary care must be taken with any manifestation of genuine alterity to the hegemonic regime. And nothing could be more alien to monotheist hegemony than polytheism, certainly not atheism. Atheism shares many structural characteristics with monotheism in the hegemonic form. Wherever polytheism raises its head to speak on its own behalf, it can expect only opprobrium, usually from every side in whatever debate is currently raging.

Let us, therefore, give the notion of polytheism some air to breathe. Rather than imposing upon it some constraining definition designed to close in and smother it as quickly as possible, let us say simply that wherever we find a cultural field in which a term easily argued to be translatable as "deity" has a plural form, and license is given within this field for directing religious regard to such deities, whether at the same time by the same worshiper, or serially by them, or simultaneously by different worshipers, that we *prima facie* find here polytheism, whether present or past.

But then we shall shortly find this little Latin phrase weaponized against the notion of polytheism as existing on any but a *surface* plane. We shall be virtually buried in assurances from every direction, and on every basis, from the ostensibly ethnographic to the purportedly logical, that any multiplicity of deities in a given field is purely phenomenal, or merely historical, or a concession to conditions of embodiment, or to the demands of social accommodation, especially of the large population of the "unenlightened." But inasmuch as there will be plenty of time for these voices to silence finally that of the Other, if they can, and given that they have already made their case over centuries and possess every organ of institutional authority, let us see if we cannot allow the phenomenon of religious regard for many Gods to articulate its own conditions of possibility, and if it is really so incoherent, to run on its own, unassisted, into whatever dead end supposedly awaits it.

In this effort, we possess some intellectual resources, and they are not meager, from Platonism, of which the entire Western tradition of thought has been termed a series of footnotes, at least when the religious affiliation of Plato and his successors is not at issue. For more important than that Plato should be Plato, is that Plato should be a monotheist. Indeed, in another of the merely apparent debates to which I referred above, no less a critic of Christianity and even of monotheism as Nietzsche refers derisively to Christianity as "Platonism for the masses." This would, however, be news to the polytheistic Platonists whose intellectual opposition was so vigorous in late antiquity as to require the services of the state to silence it through legislation in 529 CE. Only once the law prevented the unbaptized from public teaching did Platonism become safe for Christian appropriation.

In fact, Platonists had ranged themselves against monotheism going as far back as when they might first be reasonably expected to have encountered it. Plotinus, in the 3rd century CE, already wrote against those, in his day an undifferentiated assortment of Christians and others we typically term "Gnostics" today, who had in common that they "contract the divine into one".[2] Efforts to make Plato himself out to have been a monotheist stumble over the simple fact that they require us to regard as Plato's "God" things that he never termed a God, such as the Idea of the Good

---

2 *Enneads* II.9.9.36-7; see also Porphyry, *Life of Plotinus* 16.1-11. On Plotinus" critique of monotheism, see my "Plotinian Henadology," *Kronos Philosophical Journal* Vol. 5 (2016), pp. 143-159.

from the *Republic*, while disdaining as unworthy of his sincere religious regard those actual Gods, references to Whom fill the pages of his work.[3]

Moreover, these efforts toward a monotheist Plato demand that we regard his most dedicated interpreters from later antiquity, the entire tradition of systematic Platonism culminating in Proclus and Damascius, the last head of the Academy in Athens before its succession was terminated by force of law, as having perverted the tradition they alone upheld. For there was no *systematic* interpretation of Plato in antiquity that was not polytheistic, and modernity has not supplied one, since systematic interpretations of Plato have been out of fashion since the philological turn in the study of ancient philosophy in the latter 19th century.

There is a model of polytheism which has, however, cast a spell upon modern interpreters to the degree that many of them will dispute that anything differing from it ought to be considered "polytheism" at all. This model is readily identified in the poems of Hesiod and Homer and can be conveniently characterized as a division of labor, or

---

[3] On Plato's polytheism, see my "Plato's Gods and the Way of Ideas," *Diotima: Review of Philosophical Research* 39, 2011 (Hellenic Society for Philosophical Studies, Athens), pp. 73-87; see also Gerd Van Riel, *Plato's Gods* (Farnham: Ashgate, 2013).

a balancing of prerogatives. Hence Hesiod speaks of the *timai*, the "honors" or prerogatives of each God, which are allocated to them in the Olympian order established by Zeus after the resolution of the conflict of theomachy, and maintained by his powers of persuasion and his art of negotiation, though not without the potential for further conflict. The complexity of the Hesiodic or Homeric conception of such *timai* having been discarded, modern readers interpret the *timai* accorded to the Gods as essentially the same as the stereotyped "functions" with which moderns are accustomed to identify the Gods, even though the very being of a God could hardly be something accorded them in such a process of mediation. This model, due to the disproportionate influence of the poets and tragedians on our image of Hellenic polytheism, and, in turn, of our image of Hellenic polytheism upon our notions of polytheism as such, is then presented most of the time as though it is the very essence of polytheism, both by polytheism's detractors as well as by many who would defend it, at least in the abstract.

And yet we know from the careful research of those such as H. S. Versnel[4] that this model bears little resemblance to Hellenic polytheism as actually lived and practiced by worshipers. The typical

---

4 See, e.g., *Coping with the Gods: Wayward Readings in Greek Theology* (Leiden: Brill, 2011).

worshiper petitions a God less based upon what that God's "function" might be, than upon their sense of proximity to that God, the density, so to speak, of the fibers connecting them to that divine individual, at least beyond the glancing, peripheral interaction. When they approach such a divine individual, they do so generally not as though addressing a being of strictly limited power, but rather one whose power is virtually *unlimited*. And when they petition a group of Gods, it is with a sense that these Gods act in concert or at least in harmony, for the most part, and not as a field of dynamically suspended oppositional forces, as attractive as this model might be to moderns to describe phenomena to which they think the Gods ought to correspond. Furthermore, when things go wrong, even in tragedy, the ancient worshiper does not tend to blame the conflict of divine prerogatives, so much as they speak of the inscrutability and infinite depths of each divine individual or of the divine categorically.

Platonists in antiquity, who were not under the spell of this division of labor or conflict of forces model either, say that a mortal soul cannot know the number of the Gods; that there is a floor on this number, which is provided by ontology — that is, in effect, by the division of labor — but a ceiling only in the sense that the number of Gods cannot be actually infinite.[5] (This is for reasons which do not have to do with theology, but with their conception of what an actual infinity means.) Between this floor and ceiling, however, mortals have no means to determine how many Gods there are. There are, that is, at least as many Gods as there are in a given pantheon. But there are probably many more; Platonists were not given to think that only one nation had received theophany, and while some Gods might have appeared under multiple names and guises in different lands, their general approach toward such claims was reserved. Plato himself uses the names of Egyptian Gods in his writings without making any claim that they are Greek Gods in disguise,[6] though he does not mind transmitting such a claim second- or third-hand with respect to Athena and Neith.[7] Later, Iamblichus (*De mysteriis* VII.4-5) would explicitly affirm the dictum that one should not translate the foreign names of the Gods in religious texts, and the view of pagan Platonists down to the end of antiquity

---

[5] On this generally, see my "The Gods and Being in Proclus," *Dionysius* Vol. 26, 2008, pp. 93-114, esp. pp. 107ff.

[6] Thoth: *Phaedrus* 274c; Ammon: ibid., 274d; Isis: *Laws* 657b.

[7] *Timaeus* 21e.

seems to have been that the divine realm was made up of an indefinite multiplicity of living immortal individuals, the kind of entities who have proper names, rather than common nouns which may be translated from one language to another.

Moderns under the influence of the division-of-labor model, however, purport to know exactly how many Gods there are — somewhere around a baker's dozen — precisely because these are the number of divisions in an *a priori* intellectual model of the cosmos such as Jan Assmann, in his theory of "cosmotheism", thinks to be the essence of polytheism. According to such a view, the point of polytheism is not contact with individual living immortals, not theophany, but cosmology, creating a map of the forces active in the cosmos. Again, Proclus, e.g., says that a mortal soul cannot know all the properties of any God (*In Crat.* §174, 97.1-5). But moderns purport to know just what each God does, because they have reduced their identity to that of some single, discrete power which is easily defined, if not in a word, then at any rate in a paragraph.

As a result of the uncritical and almost universal adoption of this division of labor or conflict of powers model by moderns seeking to conceptualize polytheisms, ancient thinkers who do not regard this model as fundamental and feel free to critique it are taken as critical of polytheism as such, even in the absence of any explicit expression of intention on the part of those thinkers to place the Gods Themselves in question — indeed, even in the face of explicit denials that they are engaged in anything like this. A straw man of polytheism having been substituted for the genuine article, we miss the very point of what these thinkers were trying to accomplish.

For example, Plato in his *Euthyphro* makes a point of raising the issue of conflict among the Gods (7a & sqq.) in order to set the stage for his inquiry into the essence of holiness or piety. Such conflict is often considered to be inherent to polytheism and as implied by the division of labor model, it being assumed that from out of this conflict some sort of equilibrium emerges. Indeed, this is frequently praised as the very wisdom inherent in polytheism, because it expresses "Nature," and certifies the status of "paganism" as "nature religion." "Paganism" even plays a heroic role in this Romantic view, affirming deities who are "immanent" — i.e., straightforwardly identified with natural forces and having no personhood or agency — against the "transcendent" divinity of Christianity. Even beyond the fact that this view of ancient polytheisms responds entirely to modern issues and concerns, it leads to the erasure of polytheism insofar as the systemic unity of "Nature" overrides any meaningful individuality for the Gods.

Sometimes, indeed, conflict is seen as necessary even to individuate the Gods, although persons such as ourselves, notably, are not generally thought of as needing to be in conflict in order to remain distinct from one another. In the dialogue, Socrates never directly questions that the Gods do have certain conflicting values, but he does encourage Euthyphro to think harder about how to understand this conflict. The outcome of this inquiry, which lies beyond this single dialogue in the Platonic corpus as a whole, is thwarted at the outset, however, if, in the general fashion of modern commentators, we assume that Socrates regards the notion that the Gods would have differing values as a *reductio ad absurdum* of the very notion of many Gods. The *Euthyphro* draws no clear conclusions from its arguments, but it is guided throughout by the tension between the Gods having unique agency, on the one hand, while also possessing an orientation toward some sort of general cosmic good on the other, a dialectic evidently too fruitful to collapse, and which is sustained by mainstream beliefs about the Gods which we have no good reason to think that Socrates and Plato do not share. Indeed, it is clearly possible for Socrates and Plato to conceive of Gods as distinct from fixed roles, or else the question of their choice or agency could never even arise.

Another example can be drawn from Vyasa's commentary on the *Yoga Sutra* (I. 24). The commentator is explicating the verse which defines the *īśvara*, or "lord" who is the object of devotion, as "a distinct *puruṣa* [person] untouched by the vehicles of affliction, action and fruition," (trans. Rama Prasad). That is, the God as object of the devotional regard is affirmed by the *Sutra* as constituted neither by any kind of limitation or lack ("affliction"), nor by a particular pattern of activity or function ("action and fruition"). The commentator stresses further that the *īśvara* is, in his "divinity ... free from excess or equality. It is not exceeded by another divinity. Whichever is the highest, must be the divinity *īśvara*. For this reason, wherever there is the culmination of this divinity, that is *īśvara*," (Rama Prasad, p. 42).

Īśvara is hence a state which corresponds to the highest positing of divinity; but *īśvara* is for some Vishnu, for others Śiva, for others Durga, and for others some other God or Goddess. Now unless we have presupposed that this difference of worshiping this or that *īśvara* is trivial, merely contingent, which would be to dismiss polytheism itself straightaway as merely contingent, then we must rather see the whole purpose of the text as in fact freeing the space for just such unique divine individuals as these, who are to be constituted not by their functions or relations, but just as who They are, similarly to how we ourselves are regarded as unique, and not reducible to what we do or to some way in which we can prove ourselves different from everyone else. With respect to equality, the commentator continues:

> Nor is there any divinity equal to that [*īśvara*]. Because, in the case of equality, if one of the two equals says with reference to a common object of their attention, "Let this be new", and the other says, "Let this be old", then one thing only necessarily happening, unrestrained fulfillment of the wish is interfered with, and one becomes less than the other. Further it cannot be that two equals should at once possess an object desired by both. Because the wishes are contradictory. Hence he alone is *īśvara* whose divinity is free from equality or excess, and he is a distinct *puruṣa*. (Trans. Prasad, p. 42)

We should note that equality, as well as other fundamental relations like sameness and difference, likeness and unlikeness, are all negated in the First Hypothesis of Plato's dialogue *Parmenides* from applying to the One,[8] or "Unity" as such. In this fashion, the dialogue affirms that unity, that is, individuation, is not dependent ultimately upon relations. Absolute individuality is possessed by the Gods Themselves as exhibiting the highest mode of existence. Such an absolute individual, perfectly unique, would necessarily not be dependent for their existence as an individual upon being differentiated from others, nor would their uniqueness constitute in itself a substantive property that such individuals would have in common or that would render them equal, because the very sense of "uniqueness" is that it is not a property that would form a basis for comparison. Indeed, in Plato's *Timaeus* (41c), equality operates to separate two modes of divine production: the Demiurge explains that were he to create mortal souls himself, they should be equal to the Gods, but if they are created by the "Younger" Gods, that is, by the Gods who operate entirely within the cosmos, and not partially within and partially beyond it,[9] then they shall be unequal with the Gods and, by the same token, equal to one another.

---

8 *Parm*. 140b-d for Equality specifically.

9 What Proclus terms "encosmic" Gods as opposed to "hypercosmic" Gods.

Returning to Vyasa's commentary on the *Yoga Sutra*, then we can see an analogy to these Platonic reflections. Vyasa refers to a common object of two Gods' wish or will. It is the law of non-contradiction, as applied to this *object* of the Gods' intentionality, that renders equality impossible for the God *qua* God, that is, for the God in Their highest expression, as *īśvara* or "lord". Whatever is the state of affairs for cosmic beings cannot be attributed to the *īśvara* as the product of a divided will, of a division of labor, but must rather be regarded as the product of the *total* will of the *īśvara*.

We may compare this with Plato's affirmation in the *Republic* (379c-380c) that the inhabitants of the guardians' city must be taught to regard the Gods, strictly speaking, as the agents only of good in the cosmos, and hence not of everything that comes to be. This contrasts with Plato's own project as stated in the *Phaedo* (97c & sqq.) to understand *all things* according to the good. This latter project obviously supersedes the narrower project of the guardians' city. The difference between the two projects is essentially that the concept of what is good in the guardians' city is simple and worldly, and cannot sustain esoteric inquiry into the goodness of apparent evils. The guardians, accordingly, will likely be taught a theology of divided wills and perhaps even a division of labor.[10]

A total will is by definition not a partial will and not a consensus or equilibrium of wills; but who is to say that polytheism must consist of a multiplicity of partial divine wills, and not instead of *a multiplicity of total divine wills*? Of a multiplicity of finite Gods, rather than a multiplicity of infinite Gods? It is this polytheism that corresponds to the vision of the unitary agency of goodness from the *Phaedo*, and the unitary agent(s) implied by it.

We see in this fashion how texts treated by modern commentators as involving critiques of polytheism itself can instead be seen as critiques of the supremacy of the division of labor model that the modern commentators treat as synonymous with polytheism itself. In the case of the commentary on the *Yoga Sutra*, it is clear that the author is interested in a notion of divinity in which a God would be a distinct "person" (*puruṣa*) and an agent (implicit in the term *īśvara*) who is specifically *not* constituted according to such a division of labor. And we know that in fact, there were and are many such *īśvaras*. This fact *either* signifies that the state

---

10 For further commentary on the *Republic*, see my "Esoteric City: Theological Hermeneutics in Plato's *Republic*," *Abraxas: International Journal of Esoteric Studies* No. 5, 2014, pp. 95-104.

of being *īśvara* defines a different model of polytheism, which is what I have argued, or that the multiplicity of *īśvaras* must be a mere contingency. But what would give a modern interpreter license to determine that an indisputable element of the practice of a religion is merely "practical" and inessential?

If we are to avoid such interpretative arbitrariness, we must at least recognize the possibility that these authors are arguing instead on behalf of a different model of polytheism which they possess in their cultural frame of reference. This model is every bit as legitimately *polytheism* as the division of labor or conflict of powers model — indeed, more so, for the *bhakti* model is best understood as *radical* or *unqualified* polytheism, based on the pure and direct theophany of many unique Gods.

You Can't Offend the Gods

by Patrick Dunn

Hermes Ingenui

Let me tell you a quick story about how I recently "offended" a god.

This last weekend (as of this writing), I had a big party, so I moved a bunch of furniture, including the shrine I have set up to Hermes.

I, like a lot of people in this economy, have a few side gigs — royalties and investments and the like that bring in some passive income. I burn candles and make offerings on this shrine to keep that spending money churning in.

After I moved the shrine, that steady flow of pizza money suddenly stopped. For two days, I made very little from my passive income.

Then I put the shrine back up and made an offering and the money started pouring back in (well, okay, trickling — money never pours around here).

So, what do you make of that? Does that mean that, by taking his shrine down and moving it for my party, I offended Hermes? That would be one interpretation, and I know some people would agree with it.

But I don't think it's correct.

Hesiod lists a whole lot of interesting superstitions in *Works and Days*. For example, he writes, "Never step foot across the beautifully flowing waters of the ever-rushing river, until you have gazed into it, prayed, and washed your hands with clear, sweet water. Whoever crosses a river with most-wicked, unwashed hands, the gods become his enemy and bring trouble to him later," (li. 737-741, my translation). Now I don't know about you, but I don't stop at every single bridge to wash my hands and pray. Will the gods really, honestly strike out at me if I don't?

I don't think so, and here's why: The gods are perfect and unchanging, never-dying, and always happy. Being offended or angry is a human failing, not something that the gods can suffer. They are free of such weaknesses. Now I, certainly, can get offended and angry, and do from time to time, but I'm mortal. The gods probably don't lose their keys or get cut off in traffic.

Take Helios, the sun. The god gives his bounty to the entire earth, every day, all day. But sometimes, we don't receive it. We're inside, or our eyes are closed, or it's cloudy. This doesn't mean that Helios is angry at us: it just means that we are not open to receive his rays. The gods continually give their blessings. The fact that you might have rain on your picnic doesn't mean that Zeus is angry with you: it means that Zeus is giving his blessing, but you are not prepared or suited to receive it. If you were a farmer in a drought, you'd be happy with that rain.

Just as blasphemy doesn't offend the gods, offerings don't please the gods, because they're already maximally happy. The effect of offerings is on us, we ourselves. That doesn't mean we shouldn't make them: it means we should. We're not feeding the gods with our sacrifices; we're feeding ourselves.

Sallust, in *On the World and the Gods*, offers the same argument: we make offerings because they turn us toward the gods, and we avoid evil because evil turns us away from the gods. And once we're turned away from the gods, we lose their blessings. Or rather, we ignore their blessings, or misuse them. As he writes:

It is impious to suppose that the Divine is affected for good or ill by human things. The Gods are always good and always do good and never harm, being always in the same state and like themselves. The truth simply is that, when we are good, we are joined to the Gods by our likeness to them; when bad, we are separated from them by our unlikeness. And when we live according to virtue we cling to the gods, and when we become evil we make the gods our enemies — not because they are angered against us, but because our sins prevent the light of the gods from shining upon us, and put us in communion with spirits of punishment. And if by prayers and sacrifices we find forgiveness of sins, we do not appease or change the gods, but by what we do and by our turning towards the Divine we heal our own badness and so enjoy again the goodness of the gods. To say that [the gods] turn away from the evil is like saying that the sun hides himself from the blind.

What I think many pagans forget, from time to time, is that the gods are double-edged. Helios is the god of the sun, and all the good that the sun can do, but if you approach the sun unwisely, you'll end up burned or worse. Dionysus is the god of wine and freedom, but if you use your wine or your freedom unwisely, you will find that his blessings turn to curses. Apollon is the god of healing — and plague. Hephaestos is the god of fire, both of the forge that makes, and the fires that destroy. Hermes is the god of wealth and travel — and of thieves. Every god's blessing can turn to a curse, if we turn it that way through our hubris.

Hubris literally means "violence," but particularly with the idea of taking something not your own. The word is often used for a mortal who tries to usurp the power of a god, and in mythology this is often represented by the god punishing the mortal. Think of Arachne, turned into a spider because she bragged about spinning better than Athene. Or Midas, who was cursed with the ears of an ass because he tried to out-music Pan. These are just stories, and not scripture.

I hear a lot of talk about hubris from contemporary Hellenes, often with fear and trembling, as if hubris is just what we pagans call sin and we'll be punished for it by brimstone and wrath. But that's not what hubris is at all: the effects of hubris are not punishments from the gods, but a natural consequence of hubris itself.

It's really quite simple: hubris is forgetting the dual nature of the gods and thinking we can just grab all the goodies for ourselves, without regard for the essential balance of nature. It's forgetting the maxim of Delphi: "Nothing in excess." If I pour three bottles of wine down my throat, I've set myself up for the consequences because rather than recognizing the divine nature of wine and treating it respectfully, I've usurped its power for my own.

The consequences of turning away from the gods aren't just purely psychological; I think they can have actual effects on the outside world, and not always directly. Sometimes, the chain of cause-and-effect is occult or hidden. If I treat Hermes poorly enough, turn far enough away from him, I could open myself up to theft or disaster.

This doesn't mean that every single bad thing that happens to you is the consequence of some failure of piety; but it does mean that our actions have consequences. Even our spiritual actions can have physical consequences. And we can't always know for sure which consequences are the results of which actions. "Bad luck" is sometimes just that: bad luck. And sometimes it's what happens when we're not in a position to receive the constant blessings of the gods, or when we usurp those blessings through hubris.

But people get paranoid about this, and start panicking whenever, as Epictetus puts it, "a raven happens to croak unluckily." I don't think that's wise at all. Bad things happen to great pagans, and that's because we're mortal. We're subject to death and suffering, as simply part of the cosmic order of things. And sometimes the gods send us pain for a good reason, not as punishment but as training. We can find lessons in misfortune, and even build meaning out of suffering.

Did I commit hubris when I took down the shrine to Hermes? No, I don't think so, but I do think that I messed up a little bit. I turned my own consciousness away from Hermes, and closed myself down, both psychologically and physically, to his blessings. The consequences here are more occult: the chain of cause and effect isn't clear. I don't think Hermes punished me by harming my income during those two days, but I think I opened myself up to the possibility of that misfortune.

If I were going to do it again, and have to move that shrine, I'd rebuild it in the other room and leave an offering with a promise to return it to its usual place after the party. That would have kept it sacred, and would have helped keep me, I think, in pizza money for the week.

Works Cited

Epictetus, *The Enchiridion*, Translated by Elizabeth Carter, *The Internet Classics Archive*, classics.mit.edu/Epictetus/epicench.html.

Hesiod, *Works and Days*, *Perseus Digital Library*, www.perseus.tufts.edu/hopper/text?doc=Perseus:text:1999.01.0131:card=737.

Sallust, *On the Gods and the World*, n.d.

The Hellenic Gods
and the Polis

by Gwendolyn Reece

Minerva of Peace (Library of Congress)

I make no sense to myself without reincarnation.

I am a devotee of Apollon and Athena and have a strong relationship with most of the ancient Greek, or Hellenic, pantheon. I believe that this relationship comes from past incarnations, and I believe that my past lifetimes in ancient Greece range from Mycenaean times to a campaign with Alexander the Great.

The Orphic Mysteries were largely concerned with maintaining the continuity of consciousness across death and rebirth — so some of us should be remembering things. I share all of this because I want you, the reader, to have some context. I believe that I came into this incarnation with deep relationships with some of the Hellenic *Theoi* and that my perspective comes from my experiences and memories, as well as from deep research.

Several years ago, I believe I was asked by Apollon and Athena to undertake certain work for Them, namely to hold a physical space for Them in Washington, D.C. A significant part of what They want is for us to collectively take our spiritual duty as citizens of the *polis* seriously. This essay is offered in support of that aim.

The *Polis*, Politics, and the Duties of Citizenship

At least in the United States, the word "politics" has taken on a negative connotation for many. Perhaps because we are in a representative, rather than a direct, democracy, politicians can seem like their own corrupt class of professional "others" who are distant from "we, the people." At the same time, recent academic studies verify the apparent reality that the political and social polarization in the United States is extreme and that the fundamental dichotomy of all identity factors is partisanship (Iyenger & Westwood, 2015; Theodoridis, 2017). Collectively we are more concerned with "our side" winning than with functional governing. Internationally, the United States is not unique in facing these problems as we approach the third decade of the 21st century. I believe these are symptoms of an extremely serious soul-sickness in the collective life—both of my nation and in the collective life of humanity as a whole.

I define the *polis* as the communities of which we are a part. Of course, there is a historical meaning of "city-state," but when philosophers like Aristotle talk about the *polis* they often mean something more than a single type of governmental entity. Aristotle's famous comment that "man is a political animal," is not a criticism; Aristotle is not suggesting people are craven (Aristotle, 1932, p. 11). The fact that it is so often casually misinterpreted that way is an indication of our collective soul-sickness. What he means is that it is inherent in human nature to organize ourselves into groups that are larger than our blood relations and to bond together with others as societies based on mutual responsibilities. We are naturally communal. The research psychologist Jonathan Haidt (2012, p. 258), says metaphorically that humans are 90 percent chimp and ten percent bee. Individuals are not fully human if they are not engaged in their communities. This is why casting people out of their communities is so devastating, and has always been one of the most extreme forms of punishment.

Politics, then, is actually about the intersection of our individual and communal values and our responsibilities to each other and, as communities, to those outside of our immediate communities. Politics is always values-based, whether we consciously admit it or not.

From an ancient Hellenic perspective, the emphasis of citizenship is always on duty. Historically, formal citizenship was severely restricted. Since I am not trying to recreate ancient Greece, but instead am focused on rebuilding relationships with the *Theoi* and rebirthing lines of power, I believe we can appropriately reinterpret "citizenship" as the state of belonging to, of being a member of, a society — legal status aside.

What duties do we have to those with whom we share our society? What duties do we have to the institutions, norms and customs of our societies — including changing them if they are or become corrupted or counter to the good? What duties do we have to build, strengthen and maintain right relations between our society and other societies? Between our *polis* and the *Theoi*? Between our society and nature?

Throughout Hellenic cultures, there is a powerful emphasis on the duty of the citizen. If you sacrifice the good of your *polis* for personal gain or comfort, you are, by definition, not a good person. In fact, the word "idiot" comes from an ancient Greek word (ἰδιώτης) for a private citizen and was applied as an insult for people who put their personal gain above the common good.

Every citizen of a group has responsibility for the health and well-being of the group, the individuals that comprise it, and the honor of the collective. The ancient Greek term *miasma* means spiritual pollution. In the ancient texts and traditions, it is easy to find specific situations that are held to cause *miasma*, most of which are culturally specific and some of which seem to me to just be cultural taboos that uphold misogyny. But when we examine the common threads of the individual things that comprise *miasma*, we can see that *miasma* is really the spiritual pollution that results from being out of right relationship — being out of right relationship with the Gods and spirits; being out of right relationship with nature; being out of right relationship with each other through violations of Justice and duty; being out of right relationship with all of the aspects of our own nature.

I serve Apollon as *mantis*, and a tremendous number of historical oracular utterances are related to identifying *miasma* and its causes and providing the remedy. I have found something similar when He speaks through me. I was already a devotee of Apollon, but I admit that I did not fully understand how His oracular work is really another side of His role as healer until I sat and observed Him operating through me. His oracular work is often really about soul-healing for individuals who are out of right relationship, about healing collectives, and about giving counsel to avoid *miasma*.

Miasma always requires purification and healing. I believe that part of the duty of a citizen — of the member of any community — is to work to ensure that the community is in right relationship with all parties and, if necessary, to purify and heal any spiritual pollution that the society of which one is a member creates. This, frankly, is a tremendous amount of work and effort. Out of His inestimable compassion, this is part of why Apollon has asked for a center of power in the capital of the United States — to assist those of us who are striving to live as honorable citizens heal the *miasma* that we are collectively creating.

A citizen of any community is always a representative of that community and, therefore, must behave with honor or disgrace the whole. We are always ambassadors of every group of which we are a part — whether we intend to be or not — and our attitudes, actions, and words can rarify or degrade the collective.

One of the most poignant expressions of the ancient Greek concept of the duty of a citizen is encoded in the Athenian oath that was taken by the young men who were becoming citizens and entering their period of mandatory military service. On the eastern slope of the Acropolis is the cave of Aglauros, which is where this oath was taken under Her sponsorship and before numerous *Theoi*.

The oath is: "I will not shame my holy weapons, nor will I abandon my comrade wherever I take my stand. I will defend things both sacred and proper, and I will not leave my country lesser, but greater and better, both as far as I myself can, and in company with all. I will obey those who at any time exercise power reasonably, the laws which have been laid down, and those which shall in the future be reasonably laid down. If someone tries to abolish them, I will not permit it, either myself or in the company with all, and I will honor the ancestral holy things." (Kearns, 2010, p. 177).

There are a couple of critical points to make about this oath. Individual citizens are not supposed to be blindly obedient. They are always required to exercise their judgment and be sure that the orders, rulers and laws are reasonable and just. The implication is that if the individual citizen determines that the orders, rulers or laws are not reasonable or just, then it is their duty to stand in opposition to them. In ancient Athens, two of the greatest civic heroes were Harmodius and Aristogeiton — a pair of lovers who made a stand against tyranny and were martyrs for the ideals of democracy. Another important aspect of this oath is that it addresses both individual and collective responsibility. The oaths taken by Athenian jurors were similar. They required individual citizens to defend the rule of law and democracy and they swore to do so even at personal cost. That was their duty.

It is important to remember that an oath is actually a suspended curse that one lays upon oneself. Oaths are binding and the *Theoi* both witness and enforce them. The oaths taken by all the public servants in the United States are to uphold and defend the Constitution. They are not taken to swear loyalty to an individual. I believe that those *Theoi* who enforce oaths do so whether or not They are specifically invoked, because it is an expression of Their nature. Therefore, as part of my work, I call upon the Great Ones who are oath-enforcers when I believe that people who have sworn to uphold the Constitution are betraying their oaths.

The *Polis* and the Gods

While all of the *Theoi* have relationships to human collectives, there are particular Great Ones who are especially involved in the life of the *polis*. In ancient Greek prayer, the three that make up the "power chord" of ancient Greece are Zeus, Athena and Apollon. The calling that I answered from Athena and Apollon to form and hold a place and presence for Them in Washington, DC, is clearly related to Their desire to help us create a healthier and more appropriate civic life, to reclaim our duty and power as citizens, and generally to act with a greater sense of responsibility for our collectives.

Zeus Boulaios and Athena Boulaia were always invoked at the beginning of every gathering of the governing councils of the *polis*. Athena Polias is the Goddess of the *polis* and she also had an additional form or epithet that was her specific name for a particular community. In this country, I believe that Columbia is Her national form and I work with Her as both Athena Polias and Athena Columbia. I invoke Athena Columbia as the Goddess of the United States and I also call on Lady Liberty as a form of Athena as the Goddess of Democracy. Of course, the first democracy in Athens was formed under Her aegis. Zeus, Father of Gods and Men, is the God of rulers and is the upholder of the rule of law — both human and divine. Zeus holds rulers accountable to the laws of true, divine justice.

Historically and currently, Apollon is incredibly important in political life. Almost everyone knows that democracy was founded in Athens under the watchful eye of Athena. What is not as well known is the directly causal role that

Apollon played historically in the foundation of democracy as well as the creation of many of the norms and institutions that are the foundations of civic societies. One of His names is Apollon Nomimos, the Great Lawgiver. Apollon is unusual in that He speaks directly to humans through His oracles. As His Homeric Hymn says, He is the God who chooses to "prophesy for men the unerring will of Zeus" (Athanassakis, 1976, p. 19). His counsel was sought by individuals, including individual rulers, and by official representatives on great matters of state. He directed that courts be founded and that the rule of vengeance end. We know from historical records that He approved and gave counsel on the creation of constitutions, told societies to articulate rights, and insisted on the principle of *isonomia* — equality of all before the law. Very specifically in Athens, Apollon, through His oracle at Delphi, was a pivotal influence in the reforms of Cleisthenes and gave guidance on and approved the Athenian Constitution, giving birth to democracy — literally the rule of the people — for the first time in human history.

Apollon was also the guardian of young men and was the god responsible for preparing them for citizenship and instilling in them the importance of their duty. The temple of Apollon Delphinios, which is one of His forms that is also especially concerned with training citizens to undertake their duty, included the Athenian law court that would make determinations about eligibility for citizenship. Apollon Alexikaikos is the averter of all evil, and in that form, He guarded all of the places of assembly where decisions were made. Round river stones that were consecrated to Apollon Alexikaikos for protection were placed outside at the corners of the grounds of civic buildings and temples and were fed with olive oil.

Diplomats were often under the protection of Apollon and, indeed, priests of Apollon often functioned as diplomats. I believe diplomacy is often a form of healing between collectives.

Themis, Dike, and the Erinyes/Eumenides (also known as The Furies), in addition to Zeus, Athena, and Apollon, are particularly concerned with justice and with judicial systems. Themis continues to appear in our modern iconography — blindfolded, holding her scales and with her sword pointing downwards — and is often present in the courts. She embodies the principle of *isonomia*, equality before the Law. On a cosmic level, Themis and Apollon see both "what is" and "what is right," and They work to guide humanity towards the alignment of the two so that one day, they will be fully united. Dike is the daughter of Themis and Zeus and is another Goddess of Justice. Dike is particularly concerned with the manifestation of Justice in human societies. The Erinyes/Eumenides pursue oath-breakers and the guilty, thereby upholding the rule of law.

Heroes and heroines function as divine ancestors for entire groups. They often take a guardianship role over certain territory or a particular society. So, for example, Theseus was a hero of all of Attika. Aglauros, in whose cave the Athenian youth took their oaths of citizenship, is a heroine of Athens. I have personally encountered Her and during these experiences She offered to expand Her mission to promoting the ideals of civic duties in other democracies. The ideal of the *cosmopolis* — that we are all citizens of the cosmos rather than just one particular *polis* — is the ideal that drove Alexander the Great and he continues to function as a hero in promoting that principle. In many different cultures he is recognized as a hero and/or holy man and is even mentioned as such in the Koran.

Figures from modern history also continue to function as heroes, becoming consistent embodiments of ideals. George Washington and Martin Luther King Jr. are two examples — they have protective roles and move us to aspire to higher principles.

Democracy and Spiritual Evolution

It is my belief that the *Theoi* have remained in relationship with humanity, even when we were not formally worshipping Them. They have continued to inspire/in-spirit us. Athena and Apollon, who were causal in the birth of democracy in the ancient world, are also proponents of its rebirth in the modern world.

I understand this from the perspective of the role of democracy in spiritual evolution. What Athena and Apollon want from humanity is for us to collectively become fully responsible, spiritual adults. Given that there are many different ways of thinking about spiritual evolution, I want to articulate some of the foundational concepts that I hold so that you can understand where I am coming from. In particular I want to talk about group souls.

The easiest analogy is the cells of your own body. Your cells have a kind of independence. You can take them out of your body and put them in a petri dish and they can survive and have their own life. Your body is comprised of all of these individual lives that make up a type of coherence. Individual cells die and are replaced without damaging the coherence of your body, but your body would not exist without the cells. Your body experiences everything and grows and adapts through the experiences of the cells. This is also how a *polis* functions. It does not have existence without its members, yet individual members can leave or come in and the coherence is not ruptured.

Now, consider yourself as a cell in a greater body. For us, that primary greater body is the group soul that is humanity. Every one of us is a cell in the body of humanity and our experiences shape its growth and development. In turn, humanity is a cell in the group soul of this planet. The group soul of humanity is a part of the mind of the planet — not the entire mind, but a significant portion of the mind of the Greater Earth, especially the part where cognition is mixed with emotions. This Great Being in whom we live and move and have our being, like us and all life, is growing and changing — which is what I mean by evolution. The fact that this is happening on all levels of life, not just the physical, is why we call it spiritual evolution. I believe the great being that is this planet is learning and growing through the experiences of all of the group souls of which it is comprised, including the group soul that is humanity.

One of the most important characteristics of evolution is that all growth requires stimulation. There must be something that challenges the being to break through homeostasis — something that requires adaptation — and that is true whether we are talking about physical, emotional, mental or spiritual growth. The greatest periods of growth are forced by crisis and a severe crisis can result in either massive destruction or in great leaps forward. Either way, nothing is the same afterwards. I think this is what initiation actually is — it is a fundamental shift from one state of being and identity to another. In an oracular session in which I served as *mantis*, Apollon said this directly. "There is no great leap forward without the danger of a great fall." It is always this way. He also said that we cannot hold on to fear. That it does not serve us to do so. We have to keep moving, striving, and building and choosing hope.

I believe that those of us who are in various initiatory and occult traditions are among the vanguard of the group soul of humanity — meaning that we are pushing up against the bleeding edge of growth, or at least we should be if we are doing our job. Initiatory traditions are ultimately about accelerating the growth of the vanguard, usually under the care of Great Ones who care about humanity, but the process is scaffolded in order to increase our individual chances of success. So, those seeking initiations are on an accelerated track, but also have training wheels through their traditions and/or direct contact with the *Theoi* or other Great Ones. This is critical because the more of us who manage to break through into an experiential understanding of unity, the better the chance for the group soul of humanity to pass its initiatory crisis.

What I see and have been told is that humanity is in a coming of age initiatory crisis. It is my belief that the form this initiatory test will take is the climate crisis, and addressing it will require us to have true self-governance on all levels. It will require operating not as one *polis* in competition with others, but for us to work from the perspective of the *cosmopolis* and actually coordinate our efforts across all human cultures. I believe we are going to make it or we are going to die and if we fail, it will have devastating effects for the Greater Earth because we are part of the mind of this planet.

So, what does democracy have to do with spiritual evolution? It absolutely is not that it inherently leads to better government. Whether it does or not depends completely upon its citizens and, historically, it has often led to worse government than monarchy. The Nazis were legitimately elected by a democracy. We dare not forget that. But one of the key characteristics of an adult is self-governance — taking responsibility for the decisions one has to make, developing self-control, reason, deliberation, commitment, cooperation and compromise when appropriate, and dealing with the consequences of one's choices. That is what self-governance is, individually and collectively.

Democracy, when it is functioning, requires a tremendous amount from its citizens and, therefore, is one of the most powerful forms of stimulation to the group soul we can have. In our complex societies, democracy requires our citizens to broaden their perspective into trying to comprehend global issues. It requires them to understand and safeguard the structures and norms that keep democracies from becoming autocracies. In a functioning democracy, it is the duty of every citizen to understand and defend the integrity of the system and to fix it when it is broken. Imagine, for a moment, what a true, fully functioning democracy would look like and what would be required of its citizenry. I do not believe we have ever seen it on this planet, but the structures are there to support our growth if we will embrace, use and defend them.

I think it is important to point out that democracies all over the world are currently under threat of becoming autocracies, including in the United States. We each have a particular responsibility for where we are — locally and nationally. We can look at this challenge to democracies through a lens of the problems of exploitive economics or the failure of neoliberalism, or any other lens, but if all of these problems are external manifestations of humanity's internal psychological and spiritual state you will see that we are in a tremendous amount of internal conflict that needs to be addressed. If the initiatory challenge is that we must claim responsibility up to the limit of our true power, then the retreat into various forms of autocracy is a desire to avoid responsibility — avoid our duty as citizens of our communities. I suggest that part of the mass psychology of humanity is that we have tied our sense of self-worth (individually and collectively) too closely to external achievements and status. This creates a crippling fear of failure because failure then becomes an identity (I *am* a loser or a failure) rather than being an experience from which one can learn and then get on with the business of taking responsibility and fixing things. This makes humans brittle, insecure, defensive, and unable to learn.

Even though the United States is not unique in facing challenges to democracy, my personal primary responsibility is here. And the United States, at this historical moment, still has outsized influence in the world and, therefore, plays a particularly powerful role, which also means that our success or our failure will be especially potent for the entire planet. My responsibility, as a citizen of the United States, must be to the whole world, because our choices affect everyone.

The United States has a number of characteristics that are quite rare and bring with them some unusual possibilities. Except for the people of the First Nations, the bloodlines of everyone who is here trace to somewhere else. Except for First Nations' people, we are all immigrants and immigrants are our strength. Many Americans feel some ancestral loss, but the way our bloodlines are all mixed up gives us a kind of flexibility and malleability in terms of our national character that is historically rare. Although most of us are painfully aware at how we are not doing as good a job as we need to do in terms of equity and embracing our diversity, American culture is a constantly developing fusion of many cultures. We do not yet have thousands of years of parochial thought forms built into our national identity and we are blended in ways that reflect in microcosm the *cosmopolis* and are becoming ever more so.

There are, additionally, certain aspects of our national character that, when we can embrace and embody them, put us in good stead to be able to meet the initiatory crisis of humanity. It is easier to see our national character when traveling abroad, but qualities of daring, creativity, optimism, forthrightness and generosity are deeply rooted in the collective American psyche.

But there are also deep challenges inherent in the American soul. We are suffering under the *miasma*, the spiritual pollution, of the genocide of the First Nations people and of the slavery of Africans and African-Americans. I believe that we are capable of healing and purifying this *miasma,* if we can muster the courage and will to really address racism and oppression. I believe we can leverage the higher aspects of courage, daring, and forthrightness to meet this challenge, and I believe we must. Justice is not a fact in nature. It is a spiritual ideal and it is one of humanity's spiritual duties to manifest it on Earth.

I believe that we can meet this great challenge by embracing our duty as citizens of the *polis* — as citizens of our immediate communities, as citizens of our nation, and as citizens of the *cosmopolis*. I believe that it is our duty to do everything in our power, individually and collectively, to become fully responsible spiritual adults and that if we can get enough humans past an evolutionary tipping point, we will be successful in meeting our collective initiatory challenge. I believe success is possible, but not guaranteed. It is, ultimately, up to us. However, I believe we have support if we are willing to accept our duty and ask for help — and Apollon and Athena are two of the Great Ones who are ready to assist if we will try.

When my heart is overwhelmed by the enormity of the challenge that I see, I think about the metopes at the Temple of Zeus at Olympia. Each depicts one of the labors of Herakles. In one of the sculptures Herakles has taken up the burden of Atlas, holding the sky on his shoulders. He is bent over, clearly straining and giving everything He has. Behind Herakles stands Athena, effortlessly holding up most of the sky with one hand. Herakles has to do everything He possibly can, but She has the rest. So long as Herakles does His part, She will not let Him fail.

Selective Sources Consulted

Aristotle. (1932). *Politics.* (H. Rackham, Translated by). Cambridge, MA: Harvard University Press.

Athanassakis, A.N. (Translated by) (1976). *The Homeric Hymns.* Baltimore, MD: Johns Hopkins University Press.

Burkert, W. (1985). *Greek Religion*. (J. Raffan, Translated by). Cambridge, MA: Harvard University Press.

Eidinow, E. & J. Kindt (Eds.). (2015). *The Oxford Handbook of Ancient Greek Religion.* Oxford: Oxford University Press.

Flaceliere, R. (1965). *Greek Oracles.* D. Garman (Trans). New York: W.W. Norton & Company, Inc.

Fontenrose, J. (1978) *The Delphic Oracle: Its Operations and Response.* Berkeley, CA: University of California Press.

Graf, F. (2009). *Apollo.* New York: Routledge.

Haidt, J. (2012). *The Righteous Mind: Why Good People are Divided by Politics and Religion.* New York: Pantheon Books.

Iyengar, S. & S.J. Westwood. (2015). "Fear and Loathing Across Party Lines: New Evidence on Group Polarization." *American Journal of Political Science* 59(3), 690-707. http://www.jostor.org/stable/24583091

Johnston, S.I. (2008). *Ancient Greek Divination.* Malden, MA: Wiley-Blackwell.

Kearns, E. (Ed.). (2010). *Ancient Greek Religion: A Sourcebook.* Malden, MA: Wiley-Blackwell.

Konstantinou, I.K. (n.d.) *Delphi: The Oracle and Its Role in the Political and Social Life of the Ancient Greeks.* Athens: Hannibal Publishing House.

Larson, J. (2016). *Understanding Greek Religion.* New York: Routledge.

Lipsey, R. (2001). *Have You Been to Delphi? Tales of the Ancient Oracle for Modern Minds.* Albany, NY: State University of New York Press.

Parker, R. (1983). *Miasma: Pollution and Purification in Early Greek Religion.* Oxford: Clarendon Press.

Rice, D.J. & J.E. Stambaugh. (2009). *Sources for the Study of Greek Religion, Corrected Version.* The Society for Biblical Literature.

Theodoritis, A.G. (2017). "Me, Myself, and (I), (D), or (R)? Partisanship and Political Cognition through the Lens of Implicit Identity." *The Journal of Politics* 79(4), 1253-1267. https://doi-org.proxyau.wrlc.org/10.1086/692738

Of Lying Gods and True Religion

by Wayne Keysor

"Ah, what a ugly maid it is!"

It is a basic starting point in the Christian theological tradition that a true experience of God is, in all senses, true because, although the Christian god is beyond all qualities, he, or more accurately, it, embodies the highest human virtues magnified infinitely. Thus, a genuine experience of the Christian god is Truth with a capital "T," a metaphysical truth.

In the European Pagan traditions of the ancient period, this is resolutely not the case. There are many examples of divine beings, simultaneously powerful, numinous, and ultimately lying. What should we make of this potentially startling fact, considering our modern faith in these same mysterious powers?

This is not an issue to pass over lightly for it bears on the central question of the sources of religious authority within contemporary Paganism. Lying gods might pose serious problems in a religious tradition like contemporary Paganism that prioritizes the individual experience of the divine over the authority of religious tradition. For when a contemporary Pagan publicly makes claims concerning a divine will or divine characteristics and these claims have an impact on activities of the larger Pagan community, the distinction between the truth *of* a religious experience and the truth *within* a religious experience can be a yawning abyss.

So, let us begin by examining just a few, selected examples of lying gods from the ancient sources. Given the scope of this article, only a few, out of many possible examples, can be cited, but they will be enough to draw out some of the major theological issues involved with lying gods. We will begin with the Greek sources, which contain the texts least altered by Christian transmission in the European Pagan tradition, if such a unitary religious tradition might even be supposed. The three major literary sources coming out the archaic period of Greece — Hesiod's *Theogony*, and Homer's *The Iliad*, and *The Odyssey* all contain multiple references to, and descriptions of, lying gods.

Perhaps the most paradigmatic statement on lying gods in the ancient sources occurs in the opening lines of the *Theogony*. The *Theogony* is Hesiod's great epic poem on the origin and nature of the gods, and at the very beginning, before we learn anything else about the gods, we learn of their propensity to lie. The Muses tell Hesiod, the poet, who was himself a shepherd, "Shepherds of the wilderness, wretched things of shame, mere bellies, we know how to speak many false things as though they were true; but we know, when we will, to utter true things (26-28)." The Muses are the goddesses who, among other things, inspire the epic poetry from which the ancient Greeks derived their religious knowledge and more specifically, their knowledge of the gods. Given this fact, it becomes all the more remarkable that the Muses themselves speak first of lying to humans and only second of inspiring truth, and only when they will it. Furthermore, they do not even attempt to point the way to how the two might be disentangled by their human worshippers. Quite the opposite, their imperious, even derisive, tone suggests that humanity is of such low status in the eyes of the gods that we are not owed anything by them, especially not the truth.

This paradigmatic statement in the *Theogony* is underscored by examples of lying or deceptive gods in the *Iliad* and the *Odyssey*. In the beginning of Book 2 of the *Iliad*, Zeus sends a lying dream, rendered as an "evil dream," in the Lattimore translation, to the Greek king Agamemnon, in which he falsely promises him that he will sack the city of Troy the very next day (*Iliad* 2.5-35). He does this to provoke Agamemnon into renewing the attack in order to humiliate the Greeks, and by doing so, honor Achilles, who has withdrawn from the fighting in anger at an insult from Agamemnon. Zeus engages in this deception to keep a promise to Thetis, the sea goddess, who is the mother of Achilles, to the detriment of Agamemnon, who subsequently suffers defeat because he follows the urgings of the dream.

Later in the *Iliad,* after the Greeks and Trojans try to end the war by single combat, the gods intervene to drive on the slaughter by sending Athena down to the battlefield disguised as a Trojan warrior. She deceptively convinces another Trojan warrior, Pandaros, to break the truce by firing an arrow at Menelaos, playing on Pandaros' desire for glory (*Iliad* 4.68-103). The gods do this because Zeus listens to the counsel of Hera, who hates the Trojans, but in a larger sense because Troy is fated to fall to the Greeks, and the gods, regarding Troy, are agents of fate; therefore, they are carrying out the dictates of fate by extending the fighting so that the city can fall.

Both of these examples exhibit gods either lying to humans for their own purposes to the detriment of the humans, or because they are agents of fate, working out a destiny that is destructive for at least some of the humans involved.

The *Odyssey* reiterates this theme of lying gods in a different context. Athena, who is the special patron of Odysseus throughout the epic, lies or engages in deceptive actions to aid his quest to return home. In fact, the epic opens with Athena disguising herself as Mentes, a Greek chieftain and friend of Odysseus, in order to encourage Odysseus' son Telemachus to prepare for his return. She tells him of Odysseus 'plight using a carefully crafted lie intended to disguise how she obtained the information. She then goes on to manipulate him into taking certain actions to prepare for his father's return (*Odyssey* 1.105-213).

A second, particularly illuminating, example of lying gods from the *Odyssey* occurs when Odysseus washes up on the shore of his long-sought home, the island of Ithaca, confused and uncertain. Athena appears to him there in the form of an aristocratic, young herdsman, and tells him that he has arrived home. Odysseus, in response, concocts his own lie about who he is and how he came to Ithaca. Only then does Athena reveal who she truly is, praising Odysseus' ability to deceive (*Odyssey* 13.219-310). This is particularly interesting because it was not strictly necessary for Athena to lie. Arguably, she was testing Odysseus to see if he retained his cunning. For only after he lies does she reveal herself as a goddess, smiling at him, stroking his arm, and congratulating him on his ability to match the gods in deception (*Odyssey* 13.287-295). Seemingly, it is Odysseus' ability to display cunning, including outright lying when it suits his purposes, that Athena finds an admirable quality; a quality which she seems to suggest is shared by the gods. One could argue that it is precisely this quality that makes Odysseus worthy of Athena's patronage in the first place. In these two examples, a god lies first to manipulate events for the benefit of her worshipper, and then later to test his seminal virtue — praising him when he proves to be as adept at deception as the gods.

Lying gods figure into the Irish literary sources as well. The god Mannanan Mac Lir, in particular, is known for frequent deceptions. In one prominent story, he appears to the high king of Ireland, Cormac, disguised as a youth bearing a glittering fairy branch with nine red apples, which have the power to put humans to sleep and to make them forget all their woes. He sells the branch to Cormac in return for his wife, daughter, and son. Manannan then takes his family to the Otherworld, where Cormac eventually comes to recover them. After many tests, Manannan returns Cormac's family to him, but only after revealing his identity and explaining that he had tricked Cormac in order to get him to enter the Otherworld. He teaches Cormac important wisdom, and then gives him three magical objects as gifts (Gregory, 86-89).

In this example, Manannan employs deception to teach a human a positive lesson and then rewards him for his learning. And this is far from the only occasion on which Manannan lies to humans. Gregory documents a whole series of tricks played by Manannan on humans throughout Ireland in Book 4 of her *Gods and Fighting Men*. These tricks can result in momentary disaster for the humans involved, including ending up on a gallows or being killed, but Manannan eventually corrects the situation, often through magic (79-82). Manannan, as opposed to Zeus or Athena in the previous examples, seems to be mainly a benevolent liar, who either benefits humans through his deceptions or at least leaves them no worse than they were before.

In the Norse literary sources there are also many examples of lying gods. Loki is perhaps the archetypal lying god, and his stories in this regard well known. But other gods in the Norse tradition are also frequently portrayed as deceptive. Odin, the chief god, and his wife Frigga are known to deploy deception in their relations with humans. In the *Grimnismol*, Odin and Frigga make a bet regarding the hospitality of King Geirroth. To settle the bet, Odin visits the king in disguise, claiming to be a human traveler named Grimnir, in order to test the king's hospitality. However, Frigga had sent her maid-servant Fulla ahead with a false message indicating that an evil magician was coming to enchant Geirroth, who could be recognized by the sign of dogs being afraid of him (*The Poetic Edda*, 86).

Thus, when Odin arrives, and the dogs are frightened of him, he is seized and tortured by Geirroth to make him speak. Odin verbally plays with Geirroth as he is tortured, slowly revealing his identity through poetic verse, until Geirroth, to his horror, realizes what he has done and attempts to free Odin. But as he rises, he stumbles on his own sword and is run through (*The Poetic Edda*, 87-102). Once again, we have an example of gods lying to a human, and as is the case in the *Iliad*, to the detriment of the human being lied to. Geirroth seems manipulated by divine forces beyond his control and acts out of fear, which results in his own destruction.

These examples all point to the ancient understanding that one can experience the presence of the divine or receive divine inspiration that ultimately prove to be false. The experience itself is genuine, but the content of that experience is deceptive. This possibility is problematic on multiple levels.

For one, it urges us as contemporary Pagans to consider how we understand claims of religious truth. Paganism, at least in the United States, has grown up partially out of a countercultural movement that has been deeply suspicious of authority of all types. One of the major draws of contemporary Paganism is that it privileges personal experience over received religious wisdom or dogma. This can be a strength until people within the same community make rival claims, which they support with evidence derived from subjective experiences of the divine. Without accepted norms about how to adjudicate such claims, difficult conflicts can arise.

However, we do not necessarily have to accept this theological claim of ancient Paganism at face value. After all, these stories are not generally accorded the status of scripture in contemporary Paganism. They are considered neither the direct word of the gods as the Koran is in Islam nor even divinely inspired, as is Bible in Christianity. Without this kind of theological authority, one is free to argue that the ancient claim simply reflects how people experienced their gods then, as opposed to our modern experience, which is much different. It is a common theological assumption in contemporary Paganism that individuals experience the divine through their own mental lens, which is necessarily different than another's. This results in diverse types of experiences of the divine among individuals because every mind that is performing an act of interpretation is different than every other mind.

This approach is not a wholly modern innovation. Plutarch; the 1st Century CE Greek philosopher and moralist, who was also the chief priest at Delphi, argued in his *The Obsolescence of Oracles* that seers are like musical instruments that are played by the gods (9.31 and 15.65). The individual nature of the instrument matters. All instruments, though they make music, do not sound the same, and the even the same kind of instruments will sound different in the hands of different player, if they are well-strung and well-taken care of (50.1).

Another possibility to consider is that the gods may have changed since ancient times, that they once lied to humans, but no longer do. This is a live option given that both contemporary and ancient Paganism did not see its gods as existing outside the world or time, as in the case of the Christian god, who in classical theism is conceived as eternal and unchanging, a being completely beyond time. To the contrary, Pagan gods are born, and in some cases die. They can be permanently altered in physical ways by events, as for example in the case of mutilation. They can hold one social position in the cosmos at one point in time and then rise or fall in social status, depending on circumstances, at another. Given that both the physical and social status of the gods seem changeable and affected by time and circumstance, it is not a stretch to argue that the character of the gods could also change. This would allow the possibility that the gods have evolved, just as humans have, and consequently their relationships with humans have changed as well. The process theology of Alfred North Whitehead and Charles Hartshorne, adapted to a polytheistic, as opposed to monotheistic, world view might provide a theoretical framework to support such a view.

As tempting as these latter two possibilities might seem, I think it would be a mistake to abandon the theological wisdom contained in the stories of lying gods too easily. It seems to me an important recognition by the ancients that an experience of the divine is often ambiguous, even outright mysterious, and that these forces move in ways that are sometimes beyond human understanding, custom, or morality. It also encapsulates an understanding of the divine that recognizes the gods as not merely adjuncts to humans, existing solely for our benefit, but rather as having their own agendas, perceptions, and attitudes that can not only run in parallel with human interests, but also against them. All this creates a more perplexing, mysterious, and unsettling picture of the divine that mirrors the complex world that we see around us. Such a view does not allow us to lapse into easy, but false, certainties about our religious practices and experiences.

The ambiguity and complexity of our relationship with the spiritual world can be seen no more clearly in the ancient sources than in Virgil's *Aeneid*, when the hero Aeneas journeys to the underworld to speak with his dead father and see the progenitors of the Roman people. At the end of his journey, he is shown two ways to depart the underworld. *Sunt geminae Somni portae, quarum altera fertur cornea, qua veris facilis datur exitus umbris, altera candenti perfecta nitens elephanto, sed falsa ad caelum mittunt insomnia Manes (Aeneid 6.893-896). There are two gates of Sleep; of which one is said to be horn, whereby a ready exit is given by true shades; the other, shining, made from gleaming ivory, but through it the spirits of the underworld send false dreams to the upper world* (translation mine).

Aeneas leaves through the gate of ivory, the gate of lying dreams, and we are left to ponder the significance of this fact to the unfolding of the story, just as we are left to ponder the significance of lying gods in our own religious practice. So next time you take an omen or go on a shamanic journey, you just might ask yourself: Is this true? In what way is it true? And, what does the question of truth even mean to me?

Works Cited

Bellows, Henry Adams, translator, *The Poetic Edda: Translated from the Icelandic with an Introduction and Notes*. Princeton: Princeton University Press, 1936.

Boyd, Barbara Weiden, *Vergil's Aeneid: Expanded Collection*. Mundelein, Illinois: Bolchazy-Carducci Publishers, Inc., 2013.

Evelyn-White, Hugh G. translator, *The Theogony of Hesiod*. Loeb Classical Library, 1914.

Gregory, Isabella, Gods and Fighting Men. Qontro Classic Books, 2012.

Homer, *The Iliad*, translated by Richard Lattimore. Chicago, University of Chicago Press, 1951.

Homer, *The Odyssey*, translated by Richard Lattimore. New York, Harper & Row Publishers, Inc., 1965.

Plutarch, *Moralia*, translated by F.C. Babbit. The Loeb Classical Library, Vol. 5, 1936.

Moral Humans and the Immoral Gods: An Examination of the Problem of Divine Evil in Contemporary Paganism

by Wayne Keysor

Les enfants de Niobé tués par Apollon et Diane

Are the gods moral? Do they reward moral behavior in their devotees? Will they carry out evil acts at the request of their worshippers once the proper offerings have been rendered? The ancient Pagans wrestled with these questions and never settled them. They are if anything, even more unsettled in contemporary Paganism.

This struggle is in direct contrast to the newer religions of the Axial Age, typified by the varieties of monotheism developed in the Levant and the Arabian Peninsula or the distinctive South Asian religious traditions of classical Hinduism and Buddhism, which are all unabashedly moral in character. The moral life is fundamental to the achievement of personal salvation or the escape from the cycle of death and rebirth, and for all these traditions, excluding the forms of Buddhism in which deity does not play a significant role, divine beings are conceived of as fundamentally moral actors, who serve as the highest and most purified examples of the moral life.

Contemporary Paganism, which draws simultaneously on the religious traditions developed in the Axial Age and earlier polytheistic traditions, is, if anything, more conflicted than even ancient Paganism on this question, perhaps because of its clashing religious DNA.

This examination will focus first on presenting some of the debates within ancient Paganism concerning the moral nature of the gods, and then look at these ideas through the lens of contemporary Paganism. We will focus on Greco-Roman Paganism, which is the most complete version of ancient, western Paganism that is available to moderns. Unfortunately, the literary and historical sources for the other ancient, western Pagan traditions are far less intact and therefore, they present more significant interpretative difficulties.

That being said, this narrower focus is also a weakness that should be rectified in future work. The unique qualities of ancient Greco-Roman Paganism may present significant differences from other versions of ancient polytheism., The absence of discussion about those cultures makes this current project a work in progress. However, the advantage of a singular focus on Greco-Roman Paganism is that not only do we have a rich body of myth from the Greco-Roman tradition on which to draw, but also significant commentary on those stories written by Pagan intellectuals from the ancient period, as well as a solid understanding of actual, daily religious practice of ancient Greco-Roman Pagans, all of which allows us a much richer view of the question at hand.

To begin this discussion, the terms *moral* and *evil* must be defined. For the purposes of this essay, moral actors are those actors that strive for justice and whose actions are motivated by qualities such as compassion, empathy, and benevolence. In philosopher Immanuel Kant's terms, moral beings are those that treat others as ends unto themselves, rather than simply as a means to an end. We will follow Aristotle here and define justice simply as receiving that which one deserves (Lebar and Slote). Evil acts, therefore, are those acts which run contrary to morality and justice.

There are obviously problems with all these definitions, as the nature of morality and justice remains a highly contested issue in Western thought. Let it be sufficient to acknowledge that most of us share some general concepts of justice and morality, which we have attempted to capture here, although their exact nature is up for debate.

Viewpoints in Conflict: Three Motifs

Now we will consider how the ancients understood the moral character of their gods. The scholar H.S. Versnel argues quite persuasively that there were multiple competing, and logically incoherent, views of the gods and their relationship to justice, which modern scholars have struggled unsuccessfully to reconcile (151-162). Examining accounts of the actions of the gods, as they relate to justice, in the ancient Greek authors Homer, Hesiod, and Herodotus, he notes that there are clashing chords of divine capriciousness; divine justice; and inscrutable, arbitrary fate all simultaneously contained within the Greek worldview.

Caprice: Versnel's first motif shows the gods dispensing goods or evils to human beings in a manner that is not dependent on the moral character of the person receiving them, but rather is driven by the gods' own selfish whims or by other, inscrutable motivations. This motif argues that the gods are either utterly immoral, or at least largely amoral, in their relationships with human beings.

Justice: The second motif shows the gods delivering just punishment for moral wrongs committed by humans and upholding a larger cosmic order. This motif presents the gods as moral actors, at least regarding justice. (They still may be self-interested and capricious in other aspects of their relationships with humans).

Fate: The third posits a blind force that is separate from, and beyond, the gods. It is fate that assigns human beings their lot in life, whether that be good or evil; fate is not driven by any moral motivations at all. The gods themselves may be subject to the chains of fate.

Versnel observes that these three views existed in different permutations and combinations throughout the entirety of ancient Greek literature, sometimes even simultaneously in the same passages (163-187). Thus, Versnel concludes that the Greeks did not have a logically coherent view of divine justice and evil because they were struggling unsuccessfully, just as we are, to understand a world where gods existed, but suffering was ubiquitous and the just were not always rewarded (236-237).

Versnel's basic argument that there were multiple, conflicting conceptions of the moral nature of the gods among the ancient Greeks seems to accord best with the surviving source material, as well as with an empirical understanding of the psychology surrounding questions of human suffering. I would argue that these conflicting conceptions were informed, in large part, by one particular approach to deity. The ancient Greco-Roman Pagans considered their gods very human-like, an idea which has powerful implications for us as contemporary Pagans. They were human in physical form, albeit usually more beautiful and imposing. They had human-like emotions, although often magnified in intensity. They could experience anger, sadness, sexual desire, and affection. They could laugh at each other, they could have their pride offended, they could lie, and they could be cruel, an unfortunate human tendency that the gods seemed to have in spades.

The Gods in Homer: Playing Favorites

These all-too-human qualities are unabashedly on display in the two greatest epics of the Greek Pagan tradition, the *Iliad* and the

Odyssey. Just a few examples will suffice to demonstrate this point:

- The sea goddess Thetis prevails on Zeus to allow the Trojans to temporarily triumph over the Greeks out of love for her mortal son Achilles. Zeus and Hera then bicker with each other over Zeus' promise to Thetis.
- Athena and Hera fight on the side of the Greeks because their pride had been offended by the Trojan prince Paris.
- Zeus weeps tears of sorrow at the death of his mortal son Sarpedon on the battlefield.
- Apollo attacks the Greeks with his golden arrows because he feels his personal honor has been violated by the mistreatment of one of his priests.
- Poseidon is angry at Odysseus for blinding his son, the cyclops Polyphemus, and pursues an unremitting vengeance against him. Poseidon is not moved by the fact that Odysseus carried out his attack to save himself and his crew from the man-eating giant.
- Athena, on the other hand, feels a special affection for Odysseus that at times seems almost proprietary.

There are, of course, many other examples that could be cited; clearly, at this stage of development in Greek religion, there is a definite lack of what we might define as moral behavior among the gods. The gods never seem to consider the moral dimension of their decisions. They never are shown to contemplate the consequences of their actions on humans. They rarely demonstrate compassion or mercy or seem to regard humans, except for their own semi-divine offspring, as worthy of any sort of respect.

Instead, they appear to treat humans simply as means to accomplish personal ends that are important to them in the moment. In fact, if anything, the gods' interactions with humans seemed most marked by a powerful, monomaniacal selfishness that often had disastrous consequences for the humans involved. It is as if the gods embodied all the most negative traits of humanity, without our counterbalancing positive traits. This perspective leaves us with some difficult ideas to digest, as they offend our moral sensibilities and undermine our noblest hopes.

As the classicist Mary Lefkowitz argues:

The myths, as the ancient authors relate them, do not offer hope so much as a means of understanding. They enable us as onlookers to place ourselves in the world, and to get a sense of what we may reasonably expect in the course of our lives. Suffering and hardship cannot be avoided; death is inevitable; virtue is not always rewarded. Justice may not be done in the short run, although eventually wrongs will be righted, even if many innocent people will suffer There is no hope of universal redemption, no sense that in the future the victims of the terrible action of the drama will receive any recompense for their suffering (235).

Philosophy and Cosmic Justice

Indeed, this aspect of the gods in traditional myths was troubling, and the philosophers of later generations sought to address it in various ways. Such petty, immoral behavior by the gods offended the sense of the divine majesty of justice held by schools such as the Stoics and Neoplatonists. Justice was, in their view, a structural part of the cosmos.

The Neoplatonists were perhaps most influential to later Western thought in this regard, especially to Christian thought, which still exerts a powerful influence over us to this day, so let us pause a moment and consider the Neoplatonic approach to the moral nature of the gods.

Neoplatonism was a philosophical movement active from the late 3rd century C.E. to the 7th century C.E. which sought to unify many of the diverse, intellectual strains of late Greco-Roman culture into one unified, philosophical system. It posited that intelligent consciousness pre-dated matter and that all phenomena in the cosmos arose from a single, unified cause that was variously referred to as, "the First," "the One," "the All," or "the Good." And because of the first assumption, that consciousness pre-figured matter, this single, unified cause was identified as the principle of intelligent consciousness itself. Thus, all things in the cosmos emanated or arose from "the One," in stages, including, most importantly for our purposes, the gods (Wildberg). All beings existed in a great chain of being that went all the way back to "the One."

It is important to note here that, while this doctrine has some affinities with Christian monotheism, and indeed some of the doctrines of Neoplatonism made their way into early Christian thought, it is not the same thing. "The One" is not a god in the Jewish, Christian, or Islamic sense; a being that is interested in the fate of humanity and who engages in intimate, personal relationships with individuals, which are based on covenants. Rather, "the One" is completely perfect, unchanging, and fundamentally uninterested in the manifest universe, including humans. Its sole activity is contemplating the perfection of itself. Neither does Neoplatonism have a doctrine of creation, as the world is conceived of as being eternal, with no beginning. (Wildberg).

The traditional Greco-Roman gods in Neoplatonist thought were considered closer to "the One" than human beings on the chain of emanation, and thus were regarded as more perfect. This conclusion was based on the general principle that the closer a being was to "the One" on the chain of emanation, the more perfect it was *by nature*. For this reason, according the influential Neoplatonist thinker Iamblichus of Chalcis, the gods were transcendent (meaning they existed outside the material universe) and existed in the highest, most perfect state; the gods had power to do all things instantaneously; and the gods generated and governed all things without being influenced in turn by them.

This was in contrast to humanity, which, while containing the divine essence of "the One," was further away from it and therefore shared none of these signal characteristics (Shaw, 87). The goal of human life was to cultivate that divine spark and "to bring back the god in us to the divine in the All," in the words of the Neoplatonist Porphyry (Wildberg).

Fundamental to this entire discussion is the assumption that more perfect means more perfect in all ways, including moral perfection. Thus, the gods were conceived of as morally perfect beings within the Neoplatonist system. This, of course, conflicts with the older stories of the gods. The Neoplatonists, however, adapted an interpretive technique that allowed them to have their cake and eat it too. They turned to the idea of allegory as an explanation for the unethical behavior exhibited in the traditional stories. An allegorical interpretation of religious stories posits that the characters and their actions stand in for or represent larger metaphysical truths that are more than the literal action of the plot or characters. These kinds of allegorical readings are called "defensive" allegories by modern scholars. Defensive allegories are intended to defend the gods and traditional religion, while "positive" allegories are intended to illuminate philosophical doctrines, as was common practice among the Stoics, who engaged in both types of allegorical arguments (Ramelli, 337-341 and Trapp, 64).

Practice vs. Myth

Thus, we can begin to see a discomfort about the traditional stories creeping into Pagan discourse at the end of the ancient Pagan period, a discomfort that still resonates among contemporary Pagans today.

However, there is yet another way to understand the nature of the gods. Consider:

- In actual religious practice, Zeus was worshipped as a god of justice, who had a special responsibility for those who dwelled outside the protection of normal, social boundaries, including guests, strangers, and suppliants;

- The action of the *Iliad* was divinely sanctioned by Zeus, as the god who preserves the sanctity of the guest-host relationship, because Paris profoundly violated that covenant, and therefore the Greek expedition to Troy is righting a wrong (Graf, 1636-38);
- When the Greeks wanted to swear binding oaths among themselves, they did so upon the names of the gods, and the gods were expected to punish those who broke their word (Thucydides, 5.17-23 and 5.30.3-5).

So, among ancient Pagans, in practice as opposed to myth, the gods are seen to have a role in maintaining cosmic justice, an overarching justice that transcends any individual circumstance, as well as administering justice between individual people.

Unfortunately, this is only a partial solution. Even if we see some sort role for the gods in enforcing justice between people, there was no indication that the gods would ever exhibit the finer qualities of compassion, empathy, or general benevolence towards humanity without the lubricating function of sacrifice.

And then there is the dark side of Greek Paganism as it was practiced in the ancient world. It is clear there was a powerful belief that the gods, particularly the gods of the underworld; including Hermes, the escorter of the dead; Hades, the king of the underworld; his wife Persephone; Hecate, the titan associate with witchcraft and the crossroads; the Furies; and earth mother goddesses like Demeter and Gaia; would inflict harm on one's enemies, if the proper words were inscribed and the necessary ritual actions undertaken (Ogden, 44). This belief is manifested in the physical remains of curse tablets, of which we have approximately 1,600 (Ogden, 3).

Most of these curse tablets do not depend on any form of moral reasoning for their effectiveness, but rather success was based solely on the magic formulae being executed properly. There seemed to be no sense that the gods would weigh the merits of the case and decide if they would inflict harm upon someone based on moral considerations, let alone refrain from doing another harm out of a general benevolence (Odgen, 31-44). This conception of the gods shows truly frightening amoral beings, who are willing to conduct evil acts at the behest of worshippers without engaging in any moral reasoning at all.

This highly abbreviated summary of an obviously very complex subject demonstrates that the ancients held conflicting views of about the morality of their gods, depending on who was doing the interpreting and in what the situation they found themselves.

The Problem of Divine Evil in Polytheism Today

This very same thing can be said of contemporary Pagans. However, before we address the specifics of this conflict, one of the first problems we must consider when discussing the viewpoints of contemporary Pagans is the sheer diversity of the tradition. It contains everything from duotheists, to soft and hard polytheists, to pantheists, to animists, to those who worship no gods or spirits at all.

This analysis will focus on the viewpoint of hard polytheists, who are perhaps the most direct heirs of the ancient tradition, although much can and should be said on this subject from the perspective of the other streams within the tradition.

Those who are hard polytheists, or who practice an orthopraxic version of contemporary Paganism that treats deities as independent and separate beings, often speak out of two sides of their mouth on this subject. They like to look back to the ancient, western Pagan tradition and carry forward the idea of their gods as having human-like characteristics, including a range of human emotions and motivations, rather than seeing them as transcendent forces who embody universal justice and benevolence. Yet at the same time, they assume that the gods they worship are, in general, benevolent and have their best interests at heart, despite the traditional stories that seem to point to the opposite conclusion.

Indeed, few contemporary Pagans approach their religion as if their very life depended upon it, which would seem rational if one took these traditional stories seriously. These stories seem to point out again and again that a deity having human-like characteristics does not necessarily make that being benevolent, and that such benevolence is the exception rather than the rule. One needs only look at the gods invoked in the aforementioned curse tablets, looming dark and implacable, unmoved by pity or a sense of justice.

Yet at the very heart of many of the ritual forms of contemporary Paganism is the idea that the gods can be trusted to work for the good of the humans who worship them. This is not to say that this is a universal view, but it is the predominant view in my experience. One could certainly see contemporary Pagans worshiping gods, whom they considered neither good nor trustworthy, out of fear or the pursuit of power over their environment. After all, might it not be better to flatter a tyrant and potentially receive some benefits, as opposed to ignoring him and receiving nothing or worse, even if that tyrant is not dependable or good?

But for those who hold what I identify as the predominant position, how then has this circle been squared? Within contemporary Paganism, the failure of deity to exhibit transcendent good often has been replaced with a relational concept of interacting with deity. This is a conception of interacting with deity in which the worshipper and the deity form a mutually beneficial relationship with each other through repeated acts of sacrifice and gift-giving. The devotee offers up sacrifice to the deity and in return, the deity provides blessings to the devotee. This concept can be encapsulated in the ancient Roman religious formulation, *do ut des*, translated as, I give in order that you give (Thomas, 1-5).

In contemporary Paganism, the metaphor of human friendship is often used to characterize this kind of relationship. The argument goes that one of the ways that friendship grows between people is the exchange of things of value, whether that be money or time or emotional intimacy, in increasingly unselfish ways (Dangler, 20). Over time, ideally, this exchange becomes natural and, in some sense, effortless, as, in the beautiful words of Aristotle, the "friend is a second self" (1170b).

This human concept of friendship is applied analogically to forming relationships with deities. Thus, under this model, there is no need for a deity to be universally benevolent, only that he or she be willing to enter a mutually beneficial relationship with humans. Over time, this relationship ideally grows to have its own metaphysical reality that is larger than the sum of the sacrifices rendered and the blessings given, just as a human friendship can grow beyond the mere exchange of things to something deeper and more meaningful (Dangler, 20).

Implied in this model is the idea that the gods have an innate desire or inborn propensity to want to engage in these types of relationships with humans, and that our gifts have value or significance to the gods, propositions that often are left unargued or unexamined, other than to cite ancient precedent with no explanation of why this must be.

Friendship, however, is not the only analogy that contemporary Pagans draw upon to characterize their relationship with the gods. The other dominant metaphor is that of a patron-client relationship. This metaphor is based on the scholarship concerning human social relations in the ancient Greco-Roman world, and describes a mutually beneficial interaction between social unequals. The patron, who is of the higher social class, provides goods, services, and protection to the client, who is of lower social status. In return, the client provides the patron loyalty and service within his or her more limited means. In this system, a patron has many clients, allowing him to mobilize power down the various social strata of the society, while at the same time cementing the social bonds between strata (Momigliano and Cornell, 1126-27).

The ancients extended this idea to their relationships with deity, and some contemporary Pagans have taken this ancient conception of how humans interact with gods to characterize their own relationships with the gods. The gods become the patrons, as they hold higher social status, and human beings are their clients. The people give loyalty, sacrifice, and service to the gods. In return, the gods give greater blessings to the people, as befits their greater status (Thomas, 29-36).

Yet either of these relational concepts of interacting with deity pose significant problems, as they touch on the moral nature of the gods. If the gods are not fundamentally moral but are still willing to enter mutually beneficial relationships with humans, then one runs into the potential problem of forming relationships with immoral or completely amoral beings. We obviously see the problematic nature on the human plane of forming friendships with sociopaths who have no moral compass at all. They may not presently harbor ill will towards us, and in fact may be quite helpful or pleasant to us, but their lack of moral character makes them in some way unfit for the friendship of those with strong moral qualities. For one is lending aid and comfort to someone who is quite likely out in the world hurting others without any regard for the pain they are causing, which should stimulate our moral outrage.

Furthermore, it also should motivate us to wonder whether they might turn on us once we become inconvenient, as they feel no moral compunction about violating a trust if it suits their needs. These same considerations would seem apply to our relationships with deities. In fact, the gift-for-a-gift relationship is based on the unargued premise that the gods are somehow bound by either cosmic law or some internal belief to return a good for a good. If they are not fundamentally moral, as the traditional stories imply, then why would we expect them to feel bound by the principle of reciprocity? We certainly have enough experience with humans, who lack moral qualities, to know that, in these types of circumstances, reciprocity is not guaranteed, or even likely.

Possible Pathways

One way out of this thicket is to argue that the gods do not all have just one type of moral nature. This draws on the defining claim of hard polytheism, which is the proposition that the gods are all separate individuals, each with their own unique characteristics and personal qualities. Thus, it could be posited that, just as in the case of humans, some gods are highly moral in nature, some are highly immoral in nature, and many lie on a continuum in between. Under this argument, we should form relationships with deities selectively, engaging only with those deities who are fundamentally benevolent, if not always perfectly good.

How would we determine which deities are fundamentally benevolent? One answer is to engage in relationship with deities that human cultures historically have worshipped, as they have a proven track record of relating positively with humanity. This approach suggests using tradition as a guide. A second, and complementary approach, is to interact carefully with deities until we get a spiritual sense for what kind of being they each are. Using the metaphor of human friendship again, this approach is the equivalent of coming to know someone slowly, and incrementally extending your trust to them, instead of impulsively trusting them without any empirical experience to underpin this decision.

However, this is not the only overall approach we might consider to solving this problem. A second strategy might be to de-emphasize the ancient literary tradition, or to interpret these stories in terms of themes that do not necessarily speak to the individual nature of the gods as moral actors, but rather to deeper mythic truths that need to be decoded through study and contemplation. This strategy begins to take us down the path of allegory, a path trod by the ancient Stoics and Neoplatonists before us. It does not require us to embrace full spiritual allegory in the Medieval style, but it does force us to look beyond literal, character-based analyses of these stories.

Such an approach then heavily favors our contemporary experience with the gods over insights given by the traditional stories. If the community has positive experiences with a deity, in spite of morally troubling mythic narratives, it is that contemporary experience that becomes epistemologically privileged. Such an approach then challenges us in how we are supposed to relate to and use the traditional stories of the gods, if their literal meanings cannot be trusted, especially since these stories have been used by many contemporary Pagans to derive information about the personality and character of their gods. If this approach is fallacious, then the traditions that have grown up from those kinds of readings of the traditional stories would need to be reexamined.

A third strategy is to abandon the idea of human-like gods entirely or almost entirely. Under this theological approach, the traditional stories of the gods are the equivalent of funhouse mirrors, which significantly distort our view of the gods through the curving glass of the cultural assumptions and life experiences of ancient peoples. Thus, the traditional stories tell us more about ancient peoples' obsessions, fears, experiences, and expectations, than they do about the nature of the gods themselves. If the stories do provide any true sense of the gods, they do so, to borrow a biblical phrase, through a glass darkly. Here one is free to jettison the entire idea of human-like gods as presented by the traditional stories and therefore can posit benevolent gods, who are not only more powerful, but wiser, keener, and perhaps even more moral than the humans who worship them. This allows one to turn to the gods with a sense of trust because, either through an act of faith or through direct experience, the worshipper is able to trust the fundamental moral nature of the deity they worship. This is a crucial point to consider, as without such trust, worship becomes a coercive and unhealthy act for humans. Indeed, Roman intellectuals of the late Pagan period identified this very problem in human relationships with the gods by carefully opposing the quality of *superstitio* (the irrational submission to the gods) to that of *pietas* (the quality of free and rational piety). *Superstitio* was conceived of as a one-sided submission to tyrannical gods out of an irrational fear of their power, while *pietas* was a "pact freely concluded" between the gods and the human citizens of a city, which involved responsibilities on both sides, and for which both sides could be held accountable by the other (Scheid, 151, 173-176).

If we, as humans, engage in *superstitio*, then we undermine our fundamental personal dignity and moral worth, regardless of how powerful the gods might be or what blessings they might deliver. Just as we question the sycophant who serves the powerful without any sense of their own values or self-worth, so we should do the same to the person who has a similar relationship with the gods. Thus, the moral character of deities remains a very relevant question.

The problem with abandoning almost completely the traditional stories of the gods, however, is that it unmoors us from one of the main sources of knowledge about the gods that contemporary Pagans have grown to depend upon and undermines the sense of depth and continuity that results from connecting to an ancient tradition. Such an approach could be disorienting and make the community even more vulnerable than it already is to clashing interpretations of the gods without a common reference point to adjudicate these kinds of disputes, leading to even more fractures over theological questions. Furthermore, it does not, in fact, guarantee that the gods are moral actors, as belief in a thing does not assure the existence of that thing.

Where does all this leave us then? First, it is important to note that contemporary Paganism is all about diversity: diversity of opinion, diversity of belief, diversity of understanding. Therefore, it is unlikely that any one theological approach will fit all. And there is no one line of reasoning that is ultimately definitive in its ability to convince everyone. This is the normal state of theology and should not be considered a failure or a defect. After all, theology is about human exploration of the ultimate mystery, and one of the qualities that makes it ultimate is that it is not susceptible to final understandings. What ultimate mystery does allow is a series of ever-unfolding, partial or conditional understandings, which carry the seeker forward, opening new avenues of inquiry and new possibilities of living and experiencing one's faith.

Therefore, I would argue for an experiential approach to theology in solving this, and many other, theological questions. If our concern is, what is the moral nature of the gods, then we need to live our relationship with the gods to find out the answer to this question. Engage in the physical act of worship; move one's body through the arc of ritual; put on one's jacket and step out into a world full of gods with eyes, ears, and mind fully open; meditate; pray; contemplate the overwhelming beauty and terror of the cosmos; engage in theological speculation. Do all these things over and over again until they engrave upon your heart a certain meaning that is indelibly true for you. This meaning is unlikely to be permanent, or even comfortable, but it will provide a clear beacon whose light will guide you through the many wondrous unfoldings and revelations that will surely mark your passage through this world.

I, for one, through my own life's journey thus far have come to understand the divine reality, including the gods, as fundamentally a life-affirming force within the cosmos. They undergird a reality that allows life to exist and encourages its propagation. They do not contribute to the ultimate negation of life and being, but rather participate in its creation, development, and renewal. The fact that all things are in a state of continual change, but never really go out of existence constantly reaffirms for me this truth. For now, this is enough for me.

Therefore, do I ultimately know the moral nature of the gods? No. But do I pray as if I do? Absolutely.

Works Cited

Aristotle, *Aristotle in 23 Volumes, Vol. 19.* Translated by H. Rackham. Cambridge, Massachusetts, Harvard University Press, 1934.

Dangler, Michael, J. "Nine Central Tenets of Druidic Ritual." *Oak Leaves* No. 44 (Spring 2009), 20-27.

Homer, *The Iliad*, translated by Richard Lattimore. Chicago, University of Chicago Press, 1951.

Homer, *The Odyssey*, translated by Richard Lattimore. New York, Harper & Row Publishers, Inc., 1965.

Graf, Fritz, "Zeus," *Oxford Classical Dictionary 3rd Edition*. Editors Simon Hornblower and Antony Spawforth. Oxford, Oxford University Press, 1996.

LeBar, Mark and Slote, Michael, "Justice as a Virtue", *The Stanford Encyclopedia of Philosophy*

(Spring 2016 Edition), Edward N. Zalta (ed.), <https://plato.stanford.edu/archives/spr2016/entries/justice-virtue/>.

Lefkowitz, Mary, *Greek Gods, Human Lives*. New Haven, Yale University Press, 2003.

Momigliano, Arnaldo and Tim J. Cornell, "Patronus," *Oxford Classical Dictionary 3rd Edition*. Editors Simon Hornblower and Antony Spawforth. Oxford, Oxford University Press, 1996.

Ogden, Daniel, "Binding Spells: Curse Tablets and Voodoo Dolls in the Greek and Roman Worlds," *Witchcraft and Magic in Europe: Ancient Greece and Rome*. London, The Athlone Press, 1999.

Ramelli, Ilaria, "The Philosophical Stance of Allegory in Stoicism and its Reception in Platonism, Pagan and Christian: Origen in Dialogue with the Stoics and Plato." *International Journal of the Classical Tradition, Vol. 18, No. 3*, 2011. 335-371.

Scheid, John, *An Introduction to Roman Religion*. Bloomington, Indiana, Indiana University Press, 2003.

Shaw, Gregory, *Theurgy and the Soul: the Neoplatonism of Iamblichus. 2nd Ed.* Kettering, Ohio, Angelico Press/Sophia Perrenis, 2014.

Thomas, Kirk S. *Sacred Gifts: Reciprocity and the Gods: Revised Edition.* Tucson, Arizona, ADF Publishing, 2015.

Thucydides, *History of the Peloponnesian War.* London, J. M. Dent. New York, E. P. Dutton, 1910.

Trapp, Michael Burney, "Greek Allegory," *Oxford Classical Dictionary 3rd Edition.* Editors Simon Hornblower and Antony Spawforth. Oxford, Oxford University Press, 1996.

Versnel, H.S. *Coping with the Gods: Wayward Readings in Greek Theology.* Leiden, Netherlands, Brill, 2011.

Wildberg, Christian, "Neoplatonism", *The Stanford Encyclopedia of Philosophy* (Spring 2016 Edition), Edward N. Zalta (ed.), <https://plato.stanford.edu/archives/spr2016/entries/neoplatonism/>.

Appendix A: Image Credits

All images courtesy of wikimedia commons.

Aristotle by Raphael (detail from *The School of Athens*, 1509-1511)

Thoout (Thoth) Deux fois Grand, le Second Hermés by Jean-François Champollion (1790-1832). [Thoth, the Great God, the Second Hermes.]

*Plato's Academy (*mosaic in Pompeii*)*

Vyasa Grants Sanjaya a Divine Vision. Original publication credit — Author: Ramanarayanadatta astri. Publisher: *Gorakhpur Geeta Press*. Now in public domain.

Hermes Ingenui. Roman copy from the 2nd century BCE after a Greek original of the 5th century BCE. Vatican Museum.

Minerva of Peace (Library of Congress)

"Ah, what a ugly maid it is!" The god Thor disguised as the goddess Freyja, while the god Loki laughs and two cats look on. *In the Days of Giants: A Book of Norse Tales* by Abbie Farwell Brown,

illustrations by Elmer Boyd Smith. Houghton, Mifflin & Co (1902).

Les enfants de Niobé tués par Apollon et Diane by Pierre-Charles Jombert (1772). [*The Children of Niobe Are Killed by Apollo and Diana.*]

Aristotle and the Theology of the Living Immortals by Richard Bodeus

The Balance of the Two Lands: Writings on Greco-Egyptian Polytheism by H. Jeremiah Lewis

Call of the God: An Anthology Exploring the Divine Masculine in Modern Paganism edited by Frances Billinghurst

Commentary on Plato's Parmenides by Proclus

Contemporary Paganism: Listening People, Speaking Earth by Graham Harvey

Dealing With Deities: Practical Polytheistic Theology by Raven Kaldera

The Deities Are Many: A Polytheistic Theology by Jordan Paper

Devotional Polytheism: An Introduction by Galina Krasskova

The Earth, the Gods, and the Soul: A History of Pagan Philosophy from the Iron Age to the 21st Century by Brendan Myers

The Elements of Theology by Proclus

Essays on Hellenic Theology by Edward P. Butler

Essays on the Metaphysics of Polytheism in Proclus by Edward P. Butler

Essays on a Polytheistic Philosophy of Religion by Edward P. Butler

The Goddess in America: The Divine Feminine in Cultural Context edited by Trevor Greenfield

A Million and One Gods: The Persistence of Polytheism by Page duBois

On the True Doctrine by Celsus

Pagan Theology: Paganism as a World Religion by Michael York

The Path of Paganism: An Experience-Based Guide to Modern Pagan Practice by John Beckett

Plato's Gods by Gerd van Riel

Seeking the Mystery: An Introduction to Pagan Theologies by Christine Hoff Kraemer

Walking the Worlds Volume Four: Philosophy and Polytheism

Walking With the Gods: Modern People Talk About Deities, Faith, and Recreating Ancient Traditions by W.D. Wilkerson

A World Full of Gods: An Inquiry Into Polytheism by John Michael Greer

Appendix C: Our Contributors

Edward P. Butler received his PhD in Philosophy from the New School for Social Research in New York City in 2004 for his dissertation "The Metaphysics of Polytheism in Proclus." Since then he has published regularly in academic journals, edited volumes and devotional anthologies. His work focuses primarily on Platonism and Neoplatonism, on the polytheistic philosophy of religion, and on mythological hermeneutics, with significant additional focus on Egyptian theology, Hellenic theology, and Hindu theology and philosophy. He also serves on the editorial board of *Walking the Worlds: A Biannual Journal of Polytheism and Spiritwork* (ISSN 2474-3135). Many of his publications are available from his website, *Henadology: Philosophy and Theology*, which also features his online *Theological Encyclopedia of the Goddesses and Gods of the Ancient Egyptians*. He is active on Twitter @EPButler.

Patrick Dunn is a poet, linguist, Pagan, and a university English professor with a PhD in modern literature and language. His understanding of semiotics and the study of symbols arise from his training in linguistics and literary theory. He has practiced magic since childhood.

One of the most widely read writers in contemporary Occult studies, **John Michael Greer** has more than fifty books in print and blogs weekly on Ecosophia (www.ecosophia.net). An initiate in a variety of Druidic, Hermetic, and Masonic lineages, he served for twelve years as Grand Archdruid of the Ancient Order of Druids in America. He lives in Rhode Island with his wife Sara and too many books.

Michael Hardy is a writer living in the Eastern U.S., where he shares a home with his wife and a dog. He practices an eclectic spirituality centered on Hellenic polytheism and Neoplatonism. His other interests include music, travel, and good movies.

Brandon Hensley studied Russian literature at the Ohio State University, graduating with his BA in 2012. Since then he has devoted much of his time and energy into questions of Pagan theology, most of which is contained at his website, http://anexamenofwitches.wordpress.com, and questioning if he studied in the wrong field entirely. A continental realist, his focus is on the gods as real, objective beings and what it means for us to treat the gods in such a way, specifically devising a theological framework within the emerging philosophy of Speculative Realism utilizing Object-Oriented Ontology. He also amuses himself by listening to Christian missionaries and designing

Puritanical Pagan Pamphlets to (one day) pass out at the Church bake sale. He lives in Columbus, Ohio with his husband and their fur babies.

Wayne Keysor holds a Bachelor of Arts in philosophy from St. Lawrence University and Master of Arts in liberal studies with an emphasis in philosophy and religion from Notre Dame of Maryland University. He is currently studying classics at the University of Maryland College Park with a focus on the Latin language and its literature. He also has been member of Ár nDraíocht Féin, an international druid fellowship, since 2008, and has completed both basic and advanced-level coursework within that tradition. He has had numerous articles published in Ár nDraíocht Féin's journal, *Oak Leaves*, and has also published a book of religiously-inspired poetry, *The Well of Mystery*. His theological research interests lie in religious ethics, the problem of human suffering, the epistemology of religious experience, and understanding the nature of the gods.

A Witch, Philhellene, Theosophist, and Neoplatonist, **Gwendolyn Reece** has been devoted to the Hellenic deities, especially Apollon and Athena, since roughly Mycenaean times. She serves Them within the nation's capital as a priestess of the Theophania Temple, including serving Apollon as mantis. She found and recognized a place for herself in contemporary Paganism in the mid-1980s and has called herself a Witch ever since. She is a priestess of the Assembly of the Sacred Wheel and is a graduate of Caroline Kenner's shamanic apprenticeship program, Gryphons Grove School of Shamanism. She has lectured extensively for the Theosophical Society for sixteen years and held multiple leadership positions within the society. Gwendolyn is on the faculty of American University and has a strong academic background in religious studies. In addition to her work as a practitioner, she uses her academic position to conduct research on contemporary Paganism with the intention of both furthering the scholarly discourse and providing useful information back to Pagan communities.

Ptolemy Soter, the first Makedonian ruler of Egypt, established the library at Alexandria to collect all of the world's learning in a single place. His scholars compiled definitive editions of the Classics, translated important foreign texts into Greek, and made monumental strides in science, mathematics, philosophy and literature. By some accounts over a million scrolls were housed in the famed library, and though it has long since perished due to the ravages of war, fire, and human ignorance, the image of this great institution has remained as a powerful inspiration down through the centuries.

To help promote the revival of traditional polytheistic religions we have launched a series of books dedicated to the ancient gods of Greece and Egypt. The library is a collaborative effort drawing on the combined resources of the different elements within the modern Hellenic and Kemetic communities, in the hope that we can come together to praise our gods and share our diverse understandings, experiences and approaches to the divine.

A list of our current and forthcoming titles can be found on the following page. For more information on the Bibliotheca, our submission requirements for upcoming devotionals, or to learn about our organization, please visit us at neosalexandria.org.

Sincerely,

The Editorial Board
of the Library of Neos Alexandria

Current Titles

Written in Wine: A Devotional Anthology for Dionysos

Dancing God: Poetry of Myths and Magicks

Goat Foot God

Longing for Wisdom: The Message of the Maxims

The Phillupic Hymns

Unbound: A Devotional Anthology for Artemis

Waters of Life: A Devotional Anthology for Isis and Serapis

Bearing Torches: A Devotional Anthology for Hekate

Queen of the Great Below: An Anthology in Honor of Ereshkigal

From Cave to Sky: A Devotional Anthology in Honor of Zeus

Out of Arcadia: A Devotional Anthology for Pan

Anointed: A Devotional Anthology for the Deities of the Near and Middle East

The Scribing Ibis: An Anthology of Pagan Fiction in Honor of Thoth

Queen of the Sacred Way: A Devotional Anthology in Honor of Persephone

Unto Herself: A Devotional Anthology for Independent Goddesses

The Shining Cities: An Anthology of Pagan Science Fiction

Guardian of the Road: A Devotional Anthology in Honor of Hermes

Harnessing Fire: A Devotional Anthology in Honor of Hephaestus

Beyond the Pillars: An Anthology of Pagan Fantasy

Queen of Olympos: A Devotional Anthology for Hera and Iuno

A Mantle of Stars: A Devotional Anthology in Honor of the Queen of Heaven

Crossing the River: An Anthology in Honor of Sacred Journeys

Ferryman of Souls: A Devotional for Charon

By Blood, Bone, and Blade: A Tribute to the Morrigan

Potnia: An Anthology in Honor of Demeter

The Queen of the Sky Who Rules Over All the Gods: A Devotional Anthology in Honor of Bast

From the Roaring Deep: A Devotional for Poseidon and the Spirits of the Sea

Daughter of the Sun: A Devotional Anthology in Honor of Sekhmet

Seasons of Grace: A Devotional in Honor of the Muses, the Charites, and the Horae

Lunessence: A Devotional for Selene

Les Cabinets des Polythéistes: An Anthology of Pagan Fairy Tales, Folktales, and Nursery Rhymes

With Lyre and Bow: A Devotional in Honor of Apollo

Garland of the Goddess: Tales and Poems of the Feminine Divine

The Dark Ones: Tales and Poems of the Shadow Gods

First and Last: A Devotional for Hestia

Dauntless: A Devotional in Honor of Ares and Mars

Blood and Roses: A Devotional for Aphrodite and Venus

At the Gates of Dawn and Dusk: A Devotional for Aurora, Eos, and the Hesperides

The Diviner's Handbook: Writings on Ancient and Modern Divination Practices

Lord of the Carnelian Temple: A Devotional in Honor of Sobek

A Silver Sun and Inky Clouds: A Devotional for Djehuty and Set

Ascendant: Modern Essays on Polytheism and Theology

Forthcoming Titles

The Far-Shining One: A Devotional for the Spirits of the Sun

Lord of the Horizon: A Devotional in Honor of Horus

Lady of the Sycamore: A Devotional in Honor of Hathor

Among Satyrs and Nymphs: A Devotional Anthology to Hellenic Nature Spirits

Circe's Cauldron: Pagan Tales of Magic and Witchcraft

Mother of Mountains: A Devotional for Cybele and Attis

The Host of Many: Hades and His Retinue

26982874R00093

Made in the USA
San Bernardino, CA
24 February 2019